# WALKING ON EGGSHELLS

## A Couple's Journey Through Transgenderism

NOREEN ANTAO

Writers way
SOLUTIONS

# Contents

"When I first met Noreen, I was moved by how she openly embraced life. I became impressed at how her spirituality shined through her obstacles. I admire her courage and honesty. Let this book aid others to gain strength and courage to follow their path in life."
*—Evvy Frazier, Friend*

"Noreen is an excellent example of hope and spirituality overcoming all obstacles. She is a strong person, and I admire her a lot.
*—Claudia Baez – Friend*

"Noreen is an inspiration to me, and I admire her discipline working out at the gym conditioning her mind and body. My family and I love her very much."
*—Blanca Garza – Friend*

"Noreen is an intelligent, fun-loving friend who makes me laugh whenever she is around me. I admire her for producing my manuscript which made me proud."
*—Stonewall Jackson – Friend*

# Preface

Some of my dear friends are heterosexual male cross-dressers. I have attended various events with them over the years. In Dallas, there is a heterosexual male group that requires its members to be heterosexual married males. The male applicant must go through an interview and screening process.

The group welcomes and encourages their wives and significant others to participate in group events; however, very few attend. I had discussions with several of the wives and significant others as to why they didn't participate.

Responses varied, the most common being "I am uncomfortable being seen with my cross-dresser" or "I am afraid my neighbors and friends will recognize me." The genetic ladies who attend these events are usually disguised. It is not uncommon to see some of these women wearing wigs and sunglasses.

I began a quest to discover why heterosexual male cross-dressers feel different from other males. Why is it that they find more pleasure and satisfaction in dressing as females? Is it for sexual pleasure? Could it be their insecurities and disgust looking at their male organs, or are their brains wired differently from other males?

Cross-dressers coming out for the very first time are filled with joy and excitement. Some of them have waited most of their lives to wear women's clothes in public. Finally dressed as females make them extremely emotional.

Since their childhood, they dreamed of this day, and now it has become a reality. The similarity in their stories is uncanny. Most discover at a very young age they are different from other males. Their most common responses. "We are females trapped in a male body."

Our society welcomes the strides women have taken. Traditionally, women are given more leeway in their choice of clothing, jobs and hairstyles. For heterosexual males, this is not the case.

> *Deuteronomy 22:5 ESV – "A woman shall not wear a man's garment, nor shall a man put on a woman's cloak, for whoever does these things is an abomination to the Lord your God."*

# Introduction

My family were Roman Catholics born in the city of Karachi, Pakistan. We attended mass at Saint Patrick's Cathedral, which opened in April 1881 and accommodated 1500 worshippers. The Cathedral is the seat of the Roman Catholic Archdiocese of Karachi. The Cathedral is built in Gothic Revival architecture.

Now more than 100 years later, the cathedral and the grounds around it are pristinely maintained. On a given sunny day, when the rays of sunshine peek through the stained-glass windows, it lights up the Cathedral with beautiful dancing colors settling on the worshippers. Feet away from the Cathedral stands a beautiful breathtaking two-story white monument made of marble.

My parents enjoyed an excellent reputation among the priests as well as, in the neighborhood and the community. When I was very young, I remember my dad woke us up at 4:00am on a Sunday morning to attend the first mass at 5:00 am. In the winter months, he made sure we were dressed in warm gloves, scarves, knitted caps pulled down over our faces showing only our eyes and noses. My two older brothers were altar boys and served at the 5:00am mass. Once service was out, my dad took us to a bread shop and bought us a quarter-sized loaf of hardened bread with a lot of butter on it for each of us. This was our treat, and we loved it, and looked forward to it every Sunday.

In the summers, we were out of school for two months. My dad made sure to wake us up early in the mornings so we could attend mass and choir practice. In our family there was no such thing as sleeping late even on school breaks.

Alcoholism and depression were diseases that ran on my father's side. My dad and his two brothers shared the same diseases. Sadly, they continued to drink to the point of getting drunk. My dad had a very low tolerance for alcohol and after two drinks, he was unsteady on his feet with his words slurring. Even though he knew he should stop, he was unable to. He consumed the rest of the bottle until there was nothing left.

My home environment was unpredictable and chaotic. This left me in a constant state of anxiety and fear. I struggled with guilt, emotionally traumatized, low self-esteem and shame, often blaming myself for my father's alcohol addiction.

As a child, every night when he was drunk, I would hide from him, knowing what was going to happen next. Whenever he drank at night it turned him into a mean drunk. He would yell at us, call us negative names and threaten to beat us. Then he would start on my poor mum who had done nothing to deserve his yelling and cussing at her.

Every night at the age of six or seven, I lay on my bed with tears streaming down my face and fingers in my ears. I did this in attempt to drown out his yelling, asking Jesus to please make him stop. We needed to wake up early the next morning for school. My prayers were answered, as he would quit yelling, and we were able to fall asleep.

There were other families in our neighborhood who suffered with an alcoholic dad/husband. As a kid I lived in fear and did not talk about it to anyone. Partly because I felt ashamed and if I did, I was afraid it would get back to my dad.

I believe my dad suffered from depression, heart disease and high blood pressure at the time. His doctor treating him prescribed only high blood pressure medication as he claimed it would help his other ailments too. My dad like most men in his generation being treated for the same illness probably started drinking hoping, it would help ease the pain of their untreated ailments.

I was nineteen years old when my dad passed away in Karachi, Pakistan. He was almost fifty-two years old at the time. The rest of my family immigrated to the United States, four years after my dad's passing, My two older brothers were already in the United States.

My mother now had peace in an environment which was not chaotic anymore. Her children spoiled her, which hopefully made up for her suffering all those years.

Although I never intended for this disease ever to repeat itself in my life, my first marriage was to an alcoholic He turned out to be exactly like my father with domestic violence and depression. I was 9 months pregnant with my oldest son. We stopped by a department store as we needed to pick up one item needed for the baby. This was rather simple, so I rushed in and grabbed the item, I met him at the cash register and paid for it. It was an extremely hot afternoon while we walked through the parking lot towards our car. Before we made it to the car, a wave of anger came over him. He got so upset he threw the car keys under the car and began walking home.

His temper usually flared up when he was hungry or had not smoked a cigarette for a couple of hours that day. He seemed to have forgotten, I was pregnant, hot and hungry too. I wanted to go home therefore, I had no choice other than to get down on my fours to retrieve the keys from under the car. When I stood back up, there were people standing around looking sadly at me.

When I was 7 months pregnant with my second son my husband hit me so hard on the head I almost fell to the ground. My mother who was visiting me at the time was sitting by me.

We had two beautiful sons named Joshua and Jude. My husband turned out to be exactly like my dad. His choice of alcohol was beer.

Every evening, when he came home from work at 4:30pm he opened the garage door, got himself a beer from the garage refrigerator, sat on his chair overlooking the alley watching Joshua and Jude playing. His drinking did not affect our family significantly in the earlier years of our marriage. Even though he worked hard at work, and was a great handyman at home, he was always happy when we worked together on house projects.

As the kids grew older, I noticed a major change in him. He constantly nagged at us, and his consumption of beer increased dramatically. I scheduled an appointment with a doctor who told him he suffered from depression after running all the necessary tests and his drinking beer needed to be cut down drastically. The doctor prescribed him some medication for his depression; however, he refused to take it.

I suffered physical and mental abuse in his hands. His nagging increased to the point where it was unbearable. The kids became frustrated and angry with his constant yelling and his mean temper. On weekends he opened a beer at 10am or earlier and didn't stop until he fell asleep at night. It was difficult to lay beside him as the smell of the alcohol reeked through the pores of his skin.

Johsua complained to his school counselor about how his father got drunk and was physically abusive to his mum. His teacher and counselor called us in for a meeting. I sat there listening to my husband lying saying everything was okay at home. I felt ashamed of letting Joshua down and not backing up his complaint. Josuha was telling the truth. I realized then, I had become like my mum, a victim of domestic violence. I remembered asking my mum when I was seven, "mum why do you not leave him.?" In that country women did not leave their husbands even though they were abused.

One night after he consumed about ten beers, he staggered into the kitchen. He was filled with anger and could barely hold himself up. His body was tensing and had a dangerous look in his eyes. I asked him if there was anything I could do to help him with anything that was bothering him at work.

I did not realize Joshua, who at seven years old, stood beside me. My husband turned his anger on me and blamed me for all his problems. He said in a slur picked up a large metal spoon in his hand and lunged at me to shove it down my throat. I tried to grab the phone to dial 911, however I stopped when I saw a big knife in Joshua's hand. I tried to grab the knife out of Joshua's hands. I realized my son had enough of the abuse his father had put us through. He was not afraid to defend his mum. He finally stood up to his dad and said, "if you touch my mum or try to shove that spoon down her throat, I will kill you. I will go to jail as a child defending my mother, but you will be dead, and I will not worry about you ever hurting her again." My husband, even in his drunken state, was so shocked as he dropped the spoon to the ground.

We remained married for ten years. I stayed this long in the marriage as I felt my boys needed to be raised in a house with a Mother and Father. Turns out it was the worst thing I had ever done to them. My oldest son was very angry with everyone, especially me. At the age of 7 he would stand by me when his father was drunk to protect me from being hit. My son finally told us we should get a divorce as we did not get along. My younger son showed signs of emotional overload. I did not hesitate and filed for divorce. I realize now my older son was me when I was 6 years old wanting to be the protector,

I could not take the risk of him hurting me or the kids therefore, I filed for divorce.

He was by no means a dead-beat dad. He wouldn't seek help with his alcoholism, which was a major problem in our marriage. Even at death, he provided for his sons which means the world to me.

My second chance at love came when this very kind man who I met and knew immediately was the one I wanted to marry. He was a gentle and sensitive person. I felt he would make a loving husband and a great dad to my two young sons. One day my starry-eyed world turned upside down. My prince charming told me he had a skeleton buried deep down in his closet. It had been down there for thirty-three years. What he told me changed all our lives.

This book follows the ups and downs of being married to a heterosexual cross-dresser. It is my desire to tell my story with the hope it helps genetic women all over the world to pay careful attention to the signs I missed. My significant other was a cross-dresser prior to my falling in love with him. My advice to women, "if you suspect your husband or significant other may be a cross-dresser, please pay careful attention to the warning signs. My intent for being very transparent in writing this book is the hope my life experiences will help others faced with the decision, should I stay or do I distance myself as quickly as possible."

For many genetic women, the decision to stay or leave is primarily based on the pressure of living a life considered taboo by our society. These women have chosen to remain in their marriages or relationships out of love for their husbands or significant others. Not because they are weak it is quite the opposite.

These women are very strong-minded, independent, loyal, faithful, excellent and hardworking employees. Most of them seamlessly juggled careers, and families and are women of faith.

To heterosexual cross-dressers, "I encourage you to use this book as an aid in your relationships with your wives or significant others. Hopefully, this book gives you an insight into what your wives and significant others go through, when they commit and make the decision to remain in a relationship with you." Choosing to stay in a relationship with you is stressful enough, there is no reason to add additional stress to an already fragile situation.

"Parents raising children, pre-teens and teenagers in this age of gender confusion, keep the sex communication channels open as early as eleven years or earlier depending on your child's maturity level. If you do not, they are going to learn about sex from their friends at school."

These days many parents do not attend church services on Sundays on a regular basis. Some feel Sundays are the only day they get to sleep late. Believe me, I have been there however, it is the children's Christian beliefs that suffer. By the time they get to college, they are negatively influenced by their peers who will steer them toward a life displeasing to God. They are unable to defend their faith, nor have they learned how to develop a solid Christian foundation with Jesus Christ as their Savior and Protector.

# Gay Teens and Young Adults

Recently my friend's thirteen-year-old grandchild told me she liked girls not boys. As friends, we were cool with our kids talking to either one of us about the 'sex' word. I said, "ok at your age many girls don't like boys, as you grow you will start to like them." She said, "No, I mean I like girls as in 'sex' with girls." I asked her, "Do you even know what 'sex' is? Gathering from her blank stare at me, she didn't. I explained gently in graphic terms what it meant. Her eyes lit up, "No that is not what I meant to say.

"My friend at school said she was gay, all the other kids at school were making fun of her. I like her as a friend and wanted to support her so she wouldn't be so sad at school every day. Now that you know what 'sex' means, please let your young friend know she needs to have a talk with her mom or a school counselor. If she is truly gay, they can help her explore her options.

You need to quit labeling yourself or anybody else because labels hurt people especially if they are not true. If kids are making fun of other kids for whatever reason, you need to ask them to stop calling other kids names. Negatively joking at someone else's expense is just not right.

Several years ago, quite a few teenagers committed suicide. Some of these young teens grew up with dreams and feelings of being different.

Their attraction to the same sex was impossible to discuss with their families as their parent's, social circles, and churches were very homophobic. This was more common in the Asian community in the US. Their parents' position in their community is based on wealth and education. Having a child who is a cross-dresser or gay, brings shame to the entire family.

This was not the case for other teens. They came out openly and lived as gays. Their families refused to accept them, neither were they interested in having a dialog or how they could assist their children.

Instead, they turned their backs on their children, leaving them out on their own to fend for themselves. I wonder if these kids were given more love and support from their parents, would the outcome be different? Could they be heterosexual cross-dresser(s) instead of gay? I seriously doubt this would make a difference.

Some young adults tried hard to conform to what society considered heterosexual relationships as normal. They tried living as heterosexuals however, they were left feeling deprived and frustrated sexually. They ended up confessing their gay feelings and desires to their genetic partners, this understanding was not accepted well. They felt sad and responsible for the pain they inflicted on their partners. They themselves did not understand why they felt drawn and related more to gay men.

Some of these young adults finally got the courage to come out of the closet to their families, friends, and churches. They were relieved to finally get the answer as to why they felt different since there were other men like them. People accepted them openly, they were able to feel comfortable in their skin for the first time in a long time. Their personalities changed as they were happier and able to accept themselves as being gay.

# Acknowledgments

I would like to thank my heterosexual (male) cross-dresser(s) and friends for candidly sharing their experiences of living in an often-homophobic society.

To all the wives and significant others of cross-dressers I have met over the years, thank you for your love, and support and sharing your life experiences makes me humble.

My sons, Joshua and Jude, have grown to be loving, kind and accepting young adults. I am blessed and proud to have you in my life. Thanks for being so patient with me during the writing of this book.

Claudia Baez. My favorite Bartender at the Bar of Bishop for your love, support and friendship.

Evvy Frazier. You are the sister I only hoped to have; and being my sister in Christ too, makes me doubly blessed as we walk together in our love for Jesus Christ. You have always been there for me. Words cannot express my gratitude.

Thank you for consistently bringing me joy and laughter, Blanca, Marco and the rest of the Garcia sisters, Rosa. Linda and Iris. Thank you for including me in your family. I love you all.

Robert "Stonewall" Jackson (deceased). I appreciated the honor of writing your book. "The Life and Legend of Robert 'Stonewall' Jackson." You are truly an amazing young man at the age of seventy-one. I appreciate you being my personal body trainer and a very good friend.

Gus Wright. You are a true man of God. I appreciate your wisdom, rational thinking and tackling difficult issues for me. I have tremendous respect for you.

# Verbiage Homosexuality

Most people who negatively judge cross-dressers base their prejudice on their religious beliefs. Cross-dressers do not fit society's opinion of what constitutes 'normal.' I, too, struggled with my religious beliefs on this subject.

Over the years I have developed tremendous compassion for people in pain. Especially those who struggle with emotional issues.

For me it is important to consider their loving hearts and concern for each other.

Listed below are the commonly accepted definitions of words related to "Homosexuality." which can be confusing to some of us:

- **Heterosexual:** Exclusively attracted to the opposite sex **(Men/Women).**

- **Bi-Sexual:** Man or Woman attracted to both sexes.

- **Homosexual:** Exclusively attracted to the same sex **(Men/Men) Gay (Women/Women) Lesbian.**

- **Transsexual:** A person who has undergone hormone treatment & surgery to attain the physical Characteristics of the opposite sex.

- **Transgender:** Denoting or relating to a person whose self-identity does not conform unambiguously to conventional notions of male or female gender.

# Scriptures on Love & Forgiveness

It is important for us to remember Homosexuality is not an unforgivable sin. It is forgivable the same as greed, theft, murder when we turn to Jesus and repent. We receive a new life in Christ. *Acts 2:38 ESV- And Peter said to them, "Repent and be baptized every one of you in the name of Jesus Christ for the forgiveness of your sins, and you will receive the gift of the Holy Spirit.*

Christ is the new Covenant that has been promised for a very long time. If you believe and have faith in Christ, it is possible for men and women to be made new again. For all eternity without the possibility of returning to one's old self. The old is out, the new in Christ is in. *2 Corinthians 5:17 ESV- Therefore, if anyone is in Christ, he is a new creation. The old has passed away; behold, the new has come.*

This verse helps us stand in the security of knowing God's purpose for us has always been that we should become more Christ like. As Christians we must believe, if God knew us before we were born, and planned for our salvation into our eternal/permanent home with him, he certainly knows what lies ahead for us including our current trials and sufferings. This should provide us with great joy as we wait to be united with our Father forever. *Romans 8:29 ESV- For those whom he foreknew he also predestined to be conformed to the image of his Son, in order that he might be the firstborn among many brothers.*

> *Leviticus 19:18 ESV - You shall not take vengeance or bear a grudge against the sons of your own people, but you shall love your neighbor as yourself: I am the Lord.*

# The Bar at Bishop

Wednesday evenings are always the highlight of my week. I get to meet my dear friend Evvy. Blanca and bartender Claudia for happy hour at our favorite place. The Bar of Bishop in the Bishop Arts District in Dallas. Texas. My favorite frozen alcoholic beverage, Mango Suomi, is half-priced all evening long.

Evvy is a new believer in Christ. Our discussions usually revolve around how she is growing in her walk with Christ, like all new believers. Evvy faced many challenges dealing with friends and acquaintances who are non-believers. I enjoy talking to Evvy. She reminds me of myself when I first became a believer. I remember having to take baby steps to learn more about the bible. I gained knowledge by spending time in bible studies and fellowship with mature women believers in the church.

Today was a hot Wednesday afternoon in Dallas. The temperatures were already scorching with no breeze in the air for relief. It was a perfect hot afternoon for a Mango Suomi.

Since I had a few hours to kill before Evvy got to the bar, I debated on whether to go home and take a nap or head straight to the bar to visit with my favorite bartender Claudia. I always enjoy talking to Claudia who is about 5feet 5inches tall with hair down to her shoulders and is of Mexican descent. We exchange stories about how our kids are doing and the activities they participate in.

Claudia's husband also works at the bar. Sometimes when I have stayed later than usual, Jose will escort me to make sure I make it home safely. If Joshua, my son, knows I am at the bar, he will stop by and take me home. Jose, Claudia and Joshua all know I cannot handle liquor; I sit all night with my Mango Suomi or one glass of wine. After I am done with my drink, I switch to water.

The Bar won because it was closer. I decided to walk instead of driving. I am a petite lady. No more than five feet tall. I had short dark brown hair. I was wearing white jeans with a hot pink shirt open low enough to show cleavage.

I could feel the shirt hugging my body drenched in perspiration. My hair was soaking wet, and perspiration was dripping down my face. Ruining any trace of makeup, I had left. Now, at the bar's parking lot. I realized walking was a mistake. I remember thinking, "How foolish of me to walk on a hot dry Dallas summer afternoon. I'll never do this again."

As I entered the bar it took my eyes a few minutes to adjust to the dim lights that gave the place an illusion of romance. As my eyes adjusted to the dimly lit room, I spotted a couple sitting at one of the tables waiting on their food. It was still too early in the evening for people to show up. Most people usually start dwindling after they get off work around 5:30pm or later. Since I didn't see Claudia, I headed for the restroom to freshen up. I felt thankful I left an antiperspirant at the bar. It sure came in handy today.

I came out of the restroom and perched on a bar stool in my regular spot. It was always a challenge to gracefully step up on the tall bar stool since I was vertically challenged. When I finally made it on the bar stool, all I wanted to do at this point was simply relax and enjoy the cool air blowing through the vent from the ceiling above. It would have been great if I was sipping on an ice-cold Mango Suomi. I looked around for Claudia, but she was nowhere in sight.

Claudia finally emerged and was surprised to see me early in the afternoon. She poured my favorite frozen mango drink, and we spent time talking to each other.

Then she motioned me toward a lady sitting at the far end of the bar. Claudia whispered. "She is a new customer. Go introduce yourself to her, she is alone?"

I smiled. "Claudia what am I, your bar greeter now? Besides, you are the bartender. You should be talking to her." "You are the bubbly, outgoing one with a knack for putting people at ease," Claudia responded, walking off.

I am a regular at the bar. I refer to it as 'my neighborhood bar.'

Over time, I became comfortable enough I began to introduce myself to new customers. I welcomed them in and engaged them in conversation. I wanted their first visit to be enjoyable. This started a trend. Other regulars who were new followed me, welcoming newcomers to the bar.

I walked over to the new customer. As I got a closer look at her, she was an attractive lady. She flashed me with a big warm smile. I held out my hand and introduced myself, she did the same and told me her name was Jasmine.

I sat by Jasmine, and we started a conversation. Jasmine was wearing a beautiful cream silk blouse with taupe-colored flared pants and her hair was neatly braided. She was around 5 feet 2 inches tall and weighed 135 lbs. if I were to guess.

I caught Jasmine staring at my bible and my writing pad in my tote. She finally asked me, "do you always take your bible with you when you come to the bar?"

I chuckled and responded, "Evvy and I meet here on Wednesday evenings and informally discuss the bible." Jasmine said, "Noreen you are going to think I am crazy, I had no intentions of walking into this bar, I walked past it a couple of times, but something kept telling me I needed to come in. I know it was you who I was supposed to meet in this bar. I am so grateful you introduced yourself to me,""Jasmine I do not believe in chance meetings. Everyone I have met has been sent to fulfill a spiritual purpose through a divine higher power. The Holy Spirit has been trying to get your attention, I have nothing to do with the Holy Spirit that is nothing BUT GOD!!!!

"Noreen would it be okay if I joined you and Evvy here on Wednesday evenings. It has been years since I have been to church or read a bible." "Jasmine, you are welcome to visit my church on Sundays too. I belong to a bible teaching church, which you really need."

I glanced at my watch and saw it was 5:30 pm. Evvy should be leaving work now and would be at the bar in 15 minutes. Right enough fifteen minutes later, Evvy walked in. Introductions were made, and the three of us were soon chatting like old friends.

It was now 8:00 pm, and the bar did not close until 10:00 pm. I was getting extremely tired, and thankfully, we all decided to call it a night. We paid our tabs and waved goodbye to Claudia. She was busy behind the bar.

I started to walk towards home when Evvy grabbed my arm. "No way are you walking in this heat again. Let me drive you home." I was too tired to argue with Evvy. Without a fuss, I got into her car. "Now, wasn't that a lovely evening?" "It sure was Evvy." I agreed with my eyes closed.

We waited in the parking lot to make sure Jasmine was safe getting into her car and waved goodbye to her.

# Life After Divorce

The majority of my friends tell me I have an outgoing, bubbly personality. When I walk into a room, it is like a burst of sunshine just entered the room. Over the years, my life changed drastically. I learned to use humor to disguise my pain. I was successful for the most part. My friends and family had not noticed the fake smiles, and the bubbliness was simply a facade.

The trauma of growing up in a chaotic home with one parent suffering from the disease of alcoholism ended up affecting the entire family. This stigma left me with low self-esteem, feelings of inadequacy, anxiety, and depression. I successfully learned how to hide my pain and mask my hurt feelings.

When my dad or my ex-alcoholic husband hit me on the head in a drunken rage, I refused to give them the satisfaction of seeing me cry or know how hard they hit me.

Since my divorce from an alcoholic husband, I lost the desire to meet single men. My friends, of course, tried to change things for me.

One Sunday after mass my friend Debra said to me. "Why don't you join our church singles group? You will meet other divorced women learning to be single again."

"Debra!" I said, shocked. "you know I cannot do that. I am not ready to be around men just yet." "Then stay away from the men." "Make friends with the women in the group."

Debra headed to the stack of church bulletins lying on a table nearby. She picked one up and handed it to me. "Details in there. Now, make sure you at least try it out. You do not have to go again if you do not like it."

When I returned home from church, I made myself a cup of coffee and flopped in my favorite chair with the bulletin in hand. I glanced through the singles section and found an event that seemed interesting. A group was meeting at the church and had a car-pooling arrangement set up. I disliked driving long distances at night, so this seemed exactly right for me.

I called the number listed in the bulletin. A man answered. I was shaking with nervousness and could barely speak. "I am recently divorced," I managed to say. "I would like to know more about the event this coming weekend." He introduced himself to me as John. "I know you are incredibly nervous and hesitant. We all were when we first joined the group." His voice was gentle and put me at ease.

"John continued, there are several members in our group who have gone through a divorce including myself. I understand what you are going through. The members of the group will as well. "We have survived with support from others. The friendships and love we developed in this group was the therapy we all needed." Now eyes slowly starting to tear up, I said, "John. I will be at the event this weekend." "Great, we would love to have you visit us, John said." When I put the phone down, I was still shaking.

I came from a large supportive family. I had a decent job. What I needed most was to make new single friends. An abundance of church events was held on weekends. I could only attend those when my sons were visiting their dad.

I longed to have friends with whom I could take in a movie or dinner on the weekends when the boys were with their dad. However, I had just come out of a 10-year marriage and had no single friends. Most of my friends are married and busy with their own lives. However, some are still available to have dinner with me occasionally. Unfortunately, their conversations usually revolved around their marriages and date nights with their husbands. They also talked about fun monthly dinners with friends that included their husbands.

They insisted I join them, but I felt like a fish out of water at these dinners. My life has changed significantly. These conversations made me depressed. It felt like they were insensitive to my being single again.

On the night of the church singles event, I suffered an anxiety attack. The single life was so new to me. It made me vacillate between "Should I go, or should I stay home?" I paced back and forth in my living room. Eventually, with determination, I lifted my fears in prayer, asking for the courage to move on with my life. I felt calmer and my anxiety lessened. I left home and headed to the church.

When I entered the meeting room. I counted at least ten people already there. This surprised me as I expected at the most, five or six would show up. I nervously walked in and took in a brief visual of the meeting room, I had still not completely relaxed and felt a wave of anxiety coming over me. I knew the reason for the anxiety was I just realized this was my first time out alone at a social event without my husband.

The singles in the room were smiling at me. I was introduced to friendly group members. I had still not completely relaxed and felt a wave of anxiety coming over me. I knew the reason for the anxiety was I just realized this was my first time out alone at a social event without my husband.

"You will survive the divorce we all did." "We will help you put this divorce behind you. We will be with you through the healing process, and you will find happiness again." "You know there is life after divorce. You will come to this place when you are ready."

As the event ended, I had a list of names and telephone numbers. Men and women told me to call them anytime I needed something or someone to talk to. I was amazed at how comfortable they made me feel.

Some of the men who knew I had two young sons offered to include them in the group sporting events. I continued to attend group events whenever my kids were at their dad's place. I got to know a lot more singles from different parishes as well as from our church group.

There were several singles in our group who showed interest in hosting a potluck at their apartment club house. We put it on the group calendar, and we all signed up to bring a dish for the potluck.

It had been close to a year since I joined the church's single group, and I was enjoying all the events. Joshua and Jude also attended some of the events with me.

# New President Elected

I started to attend more social events on the weekends my sons were with their dad. After socializing with the group members at various events, I decided to become an active member and get more involved in the planning of events.

Jack told me an active group member, one of the previous presidents, had resigned. According to Jack the reason he resigned was because he fell in love with a group member and they planned to get married. Almost a year went by when our current president also planned to resign for the very same reason. She, too, fell in love with a group member. They planned to be married shortly.

The current president and a couple of group members approached me to discuss the election of a new president. The other members felt confident I would make a great president. "Noreen, you have great social skills, and you are very popular with the members."

I was stunned. I had only been with the group for almost a year. What were they thinking? "We feel you would make a great president," said Ricky, one of the members who came along with the president to see me. "We need someone like you to step up and take charge of our group. You have an outgoing personality. You will be successful in increasing the membership of our group."

"Also, we need to increase the participation at our group events. You are so much fun to be around, and everybody in the group already loves you." I was apprehensive but, in the end, decided to run for president. I had only one opponent in the election. Once all the votes were in. I was named the winner. I was voted in as the new president. There were quite a few jokes. "You are not going to fall in love with a group member, right? We lost our previous two presidents who married group members."

I laughed. "It has taken me ten years to get my freedom back, now why would you even think I would give it up by getting married again? I am finally enjoying being single and the freedom that comes with it."

I went back to being myself outgoing, friendly, and genuinely concerned for those suffering in pain. Making friends came naturally to me. I have always had a heart for the shy ones. I have spent a considerable amount of time helping them overcome their shyness. I understand how difficult it is for them to make friends.

At all events. I made sure to sit with the shy visitors. I gradually introduced them to a couple of members at a time. I was confident these group members would make the visitors feel comfortable.

Most of the members themselves were very shy when they first joined the group. I felt introducing the visitors to the whole group at one time could be intimidating. Not to mention overwhelming. After each event, I stayed back to speak to the new visitors. "Did you have a fun time tonight? Were you comfortable talking to the people sitting by you? The friends you made tonight, including me, would love to see you return. Call me anytime you feel shy or uncomfortable attending an event alone."

I returned phone calls from singles who had called and left messages while my kids were asleep in bed. Most of the messages were from singles needing information on the group. It was not unusual for me to spend 45 minutes on the phone convincing one single person to attend an event.

# Chicago Pizza Restaurant

One week before Halloween, I decided to host a group event. The place I had chosen was dinner at a Pizza Pallor in a neighboring town. It was further than the usual spots near the church. Events were usually centered within the church parish. The dinner event plan was based on how familiar the members were with the menu and the staff.

I picked this restaurant for its architectural design, resembling a quaint cottage. The inside of the place was uniquely designed. The dining area was split into several rooms separated by beautiful arched walls. These rooms provided a private atmosphere. The restaurant was famous for its deep-dish pizzas. They also offered a small selection of thin crust pizzas, which were my favorite.

One of our members, named Julie, was obviously not happy with my decision. "The traffic is too heavy around dinner time. Driving there stresses me out." Tall, skinny Ricky, another member chimed in. "Why don't we carpool to the restaurant? We need to venture out and try something different rather than eating at the same old places." The rest of the group agreed the pizza place was a great idea. Like Julie, I, too, did not like driving in heavy traffic.

On the day of the event everyone met in the church parking lot and piled into Ricky's van. Several of the group members decided they would drive their own cars and meet up at the pizza place. As Ricky drove into the parking lot of the restaurant, Julie was excited.

"This place looks like a cottage from one of the fairytale books I read as a child." I was glad Julie was happy with the place most of the time she was negative, and could always find something to complain about.

Ricky parked his van in one of the parking spots. He helped all the ladies out. He was such a gentleman. Ricky now stood by the entrance door, holding it open while ushering us in. I was glad I made prior reservations as the place was filling up fast.

The hostess now began seating us at our table. A server and her drink helper greeted us. They proceeded to move around the large table, taking our drink orders. We were now done with our drink orders.

A magician dressed in a black long-tailed tuxedo with white gloves and a tall black hat came by our table. He asked if he could perform some magic tricks. We all wholeheartedly welcomed him clapping and yelling. We were probably the first lively table he encountered so far.

I was pleased to see the group enjoying themselves, especially Jane. I could see her across the table, smiling at me. We exchanged smiles and thumbs up.

The magician was still performing his magic tricks through dinner and entertaining us with his humor. I am sure the generous tipping he received from his guests did not hurt him any. Ha! Ha! It had everything to do with it, lol.

# New Friend

The magic show was still in progress.

I noticed a man walking into the pizza place. He was heading straight towards our table. When he got to the table, he greeted one of the group members, Joe. Judging from the interactions between the two, it was obvious they were friends.

Joe walked over to where I was sitting to introduce his friend Jason to me. Jason was a clean-cut all-American Caucasian man standing at 5'8." He was wearing a light blue long-sleeved cotton shirt.

A quick observation of Jason's mannerisms told me he was painfully shy. Jason made little eye contact with me. I could tell he was awkward as he played with his car keys which were hanging from a chain fastened to the left side of one of the loops at the waist of his pants. The keys on this chain hung below his knee and jangled when he walked.

His casual pants, once navy blue, appeared faded and were two sizes too large for his body frame. The shoes he was wearing looked comfortable, however, could use a change. His hair color was chestnut brown. The haircut and style made him look like a young boy. I thought to myself. "I wonder if this guy knows, a different haircut and style would flatter his facial features. The eyeglasses he was wearing appeared to be heavy. The steel frames encircled thick glass lenses. The frames should have been smaller to suit his slim narrow face.

Jason was painfully shy and made little eye contact with me. when I spoke to him. He appeared to be very awkward as he was playing with his keys.

His keys were on a key ring attached to a long heavy silver chain. He had a fixed smile and if one did not know better, they would have sworn it was tattooed on his face.

He had scars on his face which were probably the result of having acne as a teenager. The scars were remarkably similar to the ones on my friend's face. My friend had acne when he was a teenager which was the result of picking at the acne. Jason's body frame was small and skinny. His physical appearance could have improved if he gained more weight.

Jason recently moved to Dallas from Maryland on a job offer. He had been living in Dallas for approximately three months. He visited the group to make new friends.

I felt drawn to Jason, which seemed strange. I hoped I would not take him on as one of my new projects to work. I already had two young sons and a stressful job. There was, however, something I saw in him that intrigued me. I could not put my finger on it just yet.

I hoped that his attending group events regularly would help him interact more quickly with other members. This would also help him not to be such an introvert. Here is a perfect opportunity to get over his shyness sooner. Jason was introduced to the people beside him, and he seemed to be at ease joining in on the conversation.

Once I had the opportunity to speak to Jason again. "Jason, I volunteered for various upcoming group events. At the meetings, different events are announced. This helped me make friends a lot sooner. I would encourage you to do the same, too.

In the group, several women were very visual when it came to men. They only dated the good-looking guys. These women were shallow and would not give Jason the time of day. They did not invest time searching beneath the skin surface for the man's heart and soul.

# Halloween Dance

That night I invited Jason and a few others to a Halloween dance held at Saint Joseph's Catholic Church. Jason politely declined the invitation, saying, "I do not wear costumes, and I don't know how to dance."

On the night of the event, I was surprised to see him. He was wearing the same clothes he wore at last week's dinner. I walked up to him, smiling.

"Where is your costume?" Jason, now smiling, said. "I'm wearing it." I returned the smile and laughed at his dry sense of humor.

The dance was held at a school gymnasium associated with the church. The place began filling up with singles from other surrounding churches. There were a multitude of people at the party wearing costumes, which were exciting to watch. Many of the singles put on their thinking caps and created some of the most amazing costumes.

The other girls and I tried to get Jason on the dance floor. "Jason, it is so simple. "We will teach you how to dance." "I have told you all I do not have any rhythm. I do not have dancing feet. They lay flat on the ground like bricks."

I was surprised he even stood up to try as he first was very adamant' He did not even want to try. Oh, my dear, he was so right. This became painfully obvious once he hit the dance floor. He just stood there trying his best to move. This only made him look more pathetic.

I felt so miserable trying to guilt him into trying. However, I was determined and refused to give up on him. "Jason I am about to stick my fingers in the belt loops of your pants. We will be facing each other. I am determined to teach you how to dance."

I stuck my fingers in both sides of the belt loops of his pants. There were other women like my friend Connie who held him upright first so he would not fall. Finally, Jason and I stood facing each other. I began swaying to the music. Jason hung on for dear life. He was a good sport and finally made some progress.

He enjoyed the attention he was getting from all the ladies. Almost all the other attendees started to cheer him on, even the guys. His confidence level was rising, and he attempted to do the Macarena. To my surprise he did extremely well. After this he was relaxed and enjoyed the rest of the evening.

The winner of the contest will be announced later in the evening. They were judging based on the most creative costume. I dressed as Betty from the Flintstones. I was truly proud of the costume I made for this event. My jewelry was crafted from the bones of the chicken we ate the night before.

The costume contest came to an end and the judges picked a winner. The winner was Nathan, a member of our group. His costume was a very tight red one-piece suit worn by professional cyclists. This was not creative.

All evening, he walked around wearing his red bike outfit with his helmet in one hand. The crowd booed at the judges. They felt other costumes were a lot more creative than Nathan's. The judges refused to change their decision. Nathan won two dinner tickets to an upscale restaurant called. The Mansion in Dallas.

# Jason's Ideal Woman

Jason and I spent more time together. Our friendship grew stronger. We became comfortable sharing bits and pieces of our personal lives. One night after a group potluck dinner Jason cleaned up the kitchen. It was now 1:00 am. Jason did not show any signs of leaving.

"Jason. I am extremely tired. I would like nothing better than to change into my PJs and get some sleep. There is a spare bedroom you can use if you plan to spend the night."

When I returned with my PJs on, I saw all the lights in the house still on, and it was not like Jason left without turning all the lights off. I walked through the house, turning off the lights. When I reached the living room, he was still sitting in the spot where I had left him earlier. He was deep in thought. I walked into the kitchen and made myself a pot of hot tea. I returned with a steaming cup of tea in hand. I sat down Indian style on my couch across from him. Finally, I asked. "What is on your mind? You obviously have something to say to me?"

He stared at me for quite a while. He was not sure if he could trust me with what he was about to say. "I joined the singles group for several reasons.

The main reason was to meet a girl. Fall in love and eventually get married. I would like to meet a woman about my height with blonde hair." In retrospect. I realized he was trying to tell me about a personal issue. He seemed to have changed his mind. Maybe he was afraid he would lose me as a friend.

# Shopping with Jason

I was disappointed listening to Jason's description of the ideal woman he wanted to meet and marry. I decided to be completely honest. "You do want to marry a blonde bombshell if I heard you correctly? If this is true Jason, you need to change the way you look and dress." He was listening. "The color of your complexion is very pale. Your shirt colors are extremely light pastels. The combination makes you look washed out. Your clothes need to suit your complexion and your size, which will make you stand out more. Wearing your pants two sizes larger. Your keys are attached to a chain hanging down from your pant loop and those worn-out shoes. They all need to go."

He laughed. "I can always find my keys when I need them. Can you say the same about yourself?" I looked at him and rolled my eyes. He laughed again.

"Okay, okay. Thank you for your advice. I appreciate it. "So, when can we go shopping? I obviously have no sense of fashion, but you seem to do?" I found myself laughing too and said. "Of course I will go shopping with you. Would this weekend work for you?"

I knew he was very tight with his money. I smiled at him and said. "It will be fun going shopping with you. I will enjoy seeing you spend your money."

We spent the next several weekends shopping for Jason. He purchased clothes, socks, and shoes. Finding shoes for Jason that fit his feet comfortably was extremely frustrating. He was very selective and fussy with the type of shoes he wore. It took us hours to visit several different shoe stores only to walk away with no purchase.

Finally, he found the shoes he liked were comfortable. He headed toward the counter with two shoe boxes in hand. "Yea! Mission accomplished, Amen." I yelled.

He looked at me and burst into laughter. The other customers who were around joined in on our laughter. They said we were hilarious. By this time, they were all aware of my dreadful shoe-shopping experience with Jason. "Why are you purchasing two pairs of shoes in the exact same style and color?" "Well, when I find comfortable shoes. I purchased two pairs. I keep the second pair as a spare when the first pair wears out." "I am so glad you are doing this. I would have to hurt you if you asked me to come shoe shopping with you again."

When we were out of the store, I turned to Jason and said, "I would suggest you replace your eyeglasses. The frames are too large and cover most of your face. The lenses are composed of glass. They are thick and heavy, have you considered wearing contact lenses?" "I am going to regret asking you for your help, aren't I?" he replied.

I completely ignored him and went on. "I will cut your hair in a style that flatters your features." "Okay. Wait just one minute, Noreen. I know you think bald men are sexy. Please do not shave me bald. I happen to like having all my hair." "No problem my friend." I smiled. "Put your head and trust in my hands." "It makes me nervous when a woman asks me to trust her. The last time I did. It was not a pretty sight." With a smile on my face, I said. "Yeah, and she was probably a blonde too. Wasn't she?" He smiled and turned his face away from me.

I cut and styled his hair. Highlighting his facial features. "What a difference a good haircut makes. Don't you think Jason?" "How would I know? I have not seen it yet?" I handed him a mirror.

"Well. What is the verdict I asked?" He looked shocked when he looked at himself in the mirror, I handed him. "I cannot believe what a difference a good haircut makes. It looks great. How much do I owe you?"

I laughed. "Don't worry you will pay for this some way or another." He grunted. "Yes, I know and that's what scares me." All the time winking at me. Previously, he had no interest in how he dressed as a man. He hid himself behind computer geek clothing, making him invisible to potential single women. With his transition completed, he portrayed an image of a successful man dressed in stylish clothes which were screaming out the words, "Look at me I am single and ready to mingle." This was a clue I should have paid more attention to.

You need to dump the London Fog overcoat you wear. It is always wrinkled and way too big for you. We need to find you one that fits you well." I could not help myself.

I started laughing. He looked at me puzzled. "What's so funny?" When I was able to compose myself enough to answer. I said. "The girls in the group say you look like Detective Colombo on the old TV show wearing that overcoat." "I happen to be fairly attached to my overcoat. I have had it for a long time. It still has life left in it.

Besides, it is wonderfully comfortable. I purchased it when I was in high school." Jason the girls already figured this out, too, and the fact you do not take it to the cleaners to get ironed. "It is always wrinkled. The age and the style are outdated."

"Hey Jason, I just remembered, the kidney foundation is coming over to pick up our donated clothing, you could add yours to our pile for them to pick up? "Please have the overcoat, your unfaded shirts and pants without holes, placed in sacks and bring them over to my home." Jason, would you like "alone time" with your London overcoat three sizes too big for you before you place it in a bag to go away,"""Say goodbye to your coat Jason."

# Valentine's Day Dance

The congregation at Saint Joseph's Church was large. Their singles group consisted of a large active number of men and women. The group planned events throughout the year.

This month they were hosting a Valentine's Day dance a week prior to February the 14th and most of our group members signed up to attend the dance.

None of the members had seen Jason after his transformation. I knew they would be startled at the change in his appearance. It was now Friday night, and I had only one more night to contain my excitement.

"Jason. For the dance tomorrow you should wear your new black shirt and black jeans." He had already decided this was what he was going to wear. He decided to annoy me. "Why do I need to dress the way you want me to?"

Unhappily, I responded. "Fine. Wear whatever you wish. I felt the black shirt against your pale skin would make you stand out, and the jeans accent your bottom well." He laughed. "I am only teasing. I planned to wear these anyway. I am only giving you a hard time."

I growled at him. "I can never tell if you are serious or joking. Your dry sense of humor can be annoying." He laughed again. "Do not lie. You love it. Your life would be boring if I were not in it." I smiled at him without responding.

The night of the Valentine's dance was finally here. I could barely contain my excitement. It was time for Jason to pick me up for the dance. He was late.

This concerned me as Jason was never late for anything. I hoped there was nothing seriously wrong. He finally showed up 30 minutes late. Even so, this puts a damper on my excitement. I was happy to see him safe with no broken bones. He looked very handsome but appeared to be frazzled.

"I am so sorry for being late. I had a tough time getting my contacts in. I almost gave up on them and wore my eyeglasses. I know how much you were looking forward to arriving at the dance early," I responded with a bright smile. "No problem. I am just glad you are okay. You look handsome. Your black shirt and jeans look great on you." "You don't look so bad yourself." he smiled back at me. "Thanks." I had difficulty pulling my dress zipper all the way up. It appeared to be stuck.

"Jason. Could you please help me with my dress zipper? I cannot get it all the way up?" I turned my back toward him. Joshua, my older son, overheard the conversation and chimed in. "Here, Mom let me help you with that."

Jason stepped back smiling, knowing fully well Joshua at nine years old thought of himself as the man of the house. Joshua tried several times but could not get the zipper to budge. He turned to Jason. "Here, why don't you give it a try?"

Jason struggled but succeeded in finally getting the zipper up as soon as the boys were picked up by their dad. We left for the dance.

The dance was held in the church gymnasium. As we entered, I looked around the room. I was hoping to get a glimpse of the group members. I was lucky as the first person I saw was Ricky. He was on the dance floor doing the tootsie roll.

"Hey there's Ricky," I called out over the music. "As you can see, he rarely has a problem finding a dance partner."

It was not difficult to spot Ricky. He was six'6' skinny, very handsome and the life of the party.

Ricky saw me and pointed me toward the table where the rest of the group members were seated.

After dodging around the dancers, we finally found our friends. Most of our friends did not recognize Jason right away. They were amazed at his transformation.

The girls who would not give him the time of day before now wanted to dance with him. He was beaming at all the attention he was getting. He looked back at me, and I smiled approvingly. He appeared self-confident yet humble with all the attention he was now receiving. We had an exciting time at the dance. Suddenly Jason grabbed my arm and pulled me toward him. My heart skipped a beat thinking he was going to kiss me.

Instead, he said "Noreen, do you remember me telling you about the contact lens I was having problems with earlier this evening." I nodded in agreement. He said, "well it just popped out of my eye, making it difficult for me to see clearly."

With the dance hall being dark there was no hope of finding his contact lens. "Jason, if we did, it would probably be flattened by the dancers' shoes." Since Jason was unable to see clearly, we decided to call it a night after visiting with our friends a little longer and said our goodbyes.

# Noreen's Potluck Dinner

My potluck dinners were usually a momentous success. This weekend was no exception. There was a higher turnout of female members at my potlucks.

Very few women attended the dinner events at the restaurants. Most were like me, single moms with a limited entertainment budget for themselves. Our earnings went to pay for our kids' needs and to pay bills to keep a roof over our heads.

The cost of babysitting was high too. To find a reliable teenager was a miracle. The moms and dads of the group always knew their kids were welcome at my home. If their kids misbehaved, the parents would need to discipline them, or they went home. Praise God, everyone behaved.

I depended on Jason's help in organizing several group activities. Being an engineer. He was always handy to have around. He was able to fix anything that was broken. He was a very honest person and if he gave you his word, he would honor it. To my excitement, one day Jason announced it was time for him to become a member of the group.

He helped me with the group potluck dinners held at my home. He had a calming effect on me. I was always stressed on the night of the potluck dinners. "Jason, if I were cooking for tonight's dinner, I would be a nervous wreck. There would be food splattered all over the stove. Is this the reason you motioned me out of the kitchen every time I came in?" Jason laughed, saying. "I am saving you that embarrassment."

"Please leave me to worry about getting the dinner ready on time. You need to do what you do best. Talk and entertain the guests as they arrive."

Jason seemed too comfortable in the kitchen and enjoyed his role as Chef. He had things in the kitchen under control. I smiled to myself as I watched Jason in the kitchen wearing my red printed apron. I admired how calm he was while cooking dinner. He had the paper plates neatly stacked on one end of the countertop; the napkins and plastic silverware lay beside the plates.

Jason loved cooking, baking cookies and preparing food to entertain guests way too much which did not bother me at first. Reminiscing of my younger days, I have grown up to be just like my mum; not very domesticated because not having the time to learn. I first learned to cook from my dad when I was 10 years old. I enjoyed spending time with my dad cooking on the weekends. I came from a family of eight which included my five siblings, mum, and dad. At an early age we all chipped in and did our share of the daily chores. My older siblings watched us when both my parents were not home which was extremely rare.

In my marriage to Jason, he chipped in and took over the domestic chores, helped the boys with their homework and attended their doctor and teacher conferences when he was able to get off work. I was traveling for business then so I could not be physically home.

My mum worked at an all boy catholic school named, St. Patrick's School. When school was out for the day, my mum rested a bit and freshened up to greet students who came over to our house for tutoring. Her tutoring sessions ended between 8pm and 9pm. Therefore, it did not seem weird to me watching Jason take on a domestic role in our marriage. My dad also worked full-time. My dad planned the meals and all six of us kids helped with the cutting, chopping, slicing of the onions frying them. Us kids prepared meals when he got home from work. My mum learned to cook in time.

Jason did not like Indian cooking, so he decided he was going to take over the cooking in our home. Joshua and Jude were thrilled with Jason's cooking.

Jason was enjoying cooking and cleaning way too much. I quickly dismissed this thought from my mind. I knew Jason was shy, and being in the kitchen kept him in the background. He was unable to keep a job, which was a red flag. In retrospect, I realized this was an important clue I should have had more concern about.

I knew breaking the news of our relationship could alarm some friends in the group. We agreed not to say anything just yet. I was happy at how successful we were at keeping this a secret.

My feet were extremely tired from cleaning the house for the potluck all day and standing on foot all evening at the party. I kicked off my high-heeled shoes, and with a glass of wine in my hand I plopped down in a sitting position on my newly carpeted living room floor. My back securely rested against the lower front edge of my Queen Anne-style couch. I was joined by my friend who seemed to have the same idea. We were engaged in a serious, deep conversation.

I was unaware Jason had moseyed his way onto the couch sitting behind me. I was startled when I felt his wrapped legs around the sides of my body. This was not very pleasant for me. I made sure Jason knew it by glaring at him. Only an hour before our first guest arrived, we went over our agreement.

"Jason, remember our agreement, no display of affection in front of the other members of the group and guests."

This was yet another clue I missed. I should have given this more attention so we could discuss it once the group members left.

If I did, maybe he would respect our agreements going forward.

Heather, an engineer, did not participate in group activities very often. Her personality was so toxic and negative that it made it difficult for others to be around her. Jason seemed the only one who she communicated with therefore, she rudely asked him, "Since when has this been going on?" Jason, like his usual self, just sat there with his tattooed smile on his face, I expected Jason to respond; however, he did not. I knew something had to be said since we had the attention of the room. Jason had no intention of responding; he continued with his tattooed smile, lol! I was left to break the news to our friends. "Jason and I are in a committed relationship." "This is yet another clue I missed. Jason could not handle confrontation."

Once the potluck dinner was over. Jason started cleaning up the kitchen. He loaded all the dirty plates, napkins and plastic silverware in large trash bags. He glanced around the house, making sure he did not miss anything. He gathered all the trash bags and took them outside with him.

I thought it strange, Jason was enjoying being in the kitchen and cleaning way too much. I quickly dismissed this thought from my mind. I knew Jason was shy, and being in the kitchen kept him in the background.

In retrospect, I realized this was an important clue I should have had more concern about.

# The Café For Brunch

Most of the group members attended mass on Sunday mornings. We sat together in the same church pew during mass. After mass we met at a predetermined restaurant for brunch. I always wondered why Jason did not attend church on Sundays. I excused this behavior; he just wanted to sleep late.

At one of our monthly meetings. Chad, a recently divorced member of the group, asked Jason. "Hey, Jason, are you going to meet us at mass this Sunday? After mass, we will be going to brunch at the new little café down the street. Everyone says it is the best new café in town." Jason smiled. "I am not sure if I will be at mass. I will try to meet the group for brunch." This conversation was soon forgotten as the agenda for that evening's meeting was passed around the table. The meeting began with me leading the group in prayer.

The following Sunday after mass the group headed to their cars and drove to the little café down the street for brunch. When we got to the café Oscar the owner greeted us. The group members recognized Oscar as an inactive member of the group for the past two years. Oscar was glad to see everybody again. He personally escorted us to a table large enough to seat all of us. There was room to add more chairs if necessary. I was introduced to Oscar. He pulled out a chair and waited till I sat down.

Oscar was a dark-skinned, handsome man around five'9." His body was muscular and toned. He seemed to take an interest in me. He said, "I moved from Columbia to Dallas seventeen years ago on a job offer. My company later sponsored me to become a US citizen. I stayed with the company for fifteen years. Two years ago. I decided to start my own business." I gathered from the sequels from the women. Oscar had a lot of admirers.

I gazed around the café which was not overly decorated. It did not have all the bells and whistles like other surrounding restaurants. The dining area and the bathrooms were very clean.

Once everybody was seated, the server came over to take drink orders. Most of the women ordered sweet, iced tea. The men ordered the café's house beer. The beer was claimed to be the best beer in town.

To everyone's surprise. Jason joined the group for brunch. He sat by me and my heart skipped a beat as Jason was getting comfortable in his seat. Oscar came to the table with a drink. He said. "For the beautiful lady," deliberately speaking in a thick Columbian accent. It was a cool iced drink made of tequila and coconut milk. Jason said. "Hey, Noreen. How do you know that drink is for you and not me?" "Jason, " he said to a beautiful lady. I am the only lady sitting between you and Chad." In retrospect, I realized Jason was trying to give me a hint that I did not catch.

Chad asked Jason. "How come you did not make it to mass? Did you sleep in?" Jason replied. "No, I didn't sleep in." Chad was not about to let this drop. "Then why were you not at mass?"

Jason, now irritated, responded. "I guess my earlier response did not satisfy you. I am not Catholic. I am Methodist. That is why I do not attend mass."

There was a pin-drop silence. It seemed to last forever. I broke out in laughter. The rest of the members joined in except Chad who looked confused. Once the laughter stopped, I said. "Hey, we are a Catholic singles group. How did you manage to squeeze in without any of us knowing you were Methodist?

Jason just smiled and responded very quietly in my ear. "You will never know." This time, my heart skipped a beat of foreboding as we were leaving the café. Oscar walked over to me. "Thank you for coming. I hope to see you again, right?"

I smiled at him and said. "The food was delicious, and the service was excellent."

# Falling in Love

Since we were spending so much time together, it was no surprise we fell in love. I was a short, petite woman who did not quite make it to five feet.

My skin color was a deep tan, with short brown hair. I was the opposite of what Jason thought he was looking for in a woman.

I jokingly asked him. "Should I wear a blonde wig to be the blonde bombshell you were hoping to fall in love with?" "That will not be necessary. I love you just the way you are."

Falling in love so soon after my divorce scared me. It was hard not to remember how unhappy I was in my previous relationship. I questioned whether it was too soon to be in a committed relationship.

I knew Jason loved the boys and having his own family was so important to him. The kids were just at the right age where they could enhance their computer skills. Work on weird science projects and build a wooden fort with a sandbox under it for them to play in. He expressed his disinterest in having little babies of his own. The thought of changing diapers and waking up at odd times in the night to hungry infants was not appealing to him whatsoever.

Leaving the boys alone with Jason scared me. Crazy thoughts raced through my mind. "What if he was a child molester? What if he physically abused the boys when I was not around?"

To ease my mind, I decided to test him. On several occasions, I would leave the boys home alone with him. "Dear, I have some errands to run. Do you mind watching the boys until I get back? I should not be gone more than an hour or so." "Take your time dear. We three boys will have a good time together here."

When I got home, he and the boys were busy playing a game on the computer. They were unaware I was even home. This really made me happy seeing Jason so comfortable with the boys. The boys were enjoying his attention focused on them.

# Lunch Invitation

My friends from work who had earlier met Jason were surprised at his transformation, too. They were aware of the seriousness of my relationship with him. They were already picking out bridesmaid's dresses from a bridal catalog they had in the office. I tried to stop this by reminding them he had not yet asked me to marry him.

Jason unexpectedly came by the office to invite me to lunch. My office door was open and faced the main entrance door to the suite. There was no time to hide the bridal magazine. He caught my friends flipping through the magazine in my office. "I see you all looking through a bridal magazine. Which one of you is getting married?" He grinned.

They smiled at him saying. "We are just looking as you never know one of us may need ideas for our wedding. All we would then need is a wedding proposal from a very nice guy." Their eyes turned towards me. I was so embarrassed. Finally, I turned to Jason and said. "I accept your lunch invitation Jason. Can we please leave now?" At this point. I was head over heels in love with him and was extremely happy.

While at lunch I mused. "I cannot imagine anything ruining the love we have for each other. Do you? He did not respond. This was also a huge clue I missed.

When I returned to the office after lunch there was a huge bouquet of yellow roses sitting on a desk a few feet away from my office. The card on it read "Noreen, Thanks for a beautiful weekend! My co-workers kept teasing me, "Hey, Christian lady." what happened to "I will wait till I get married again," "What did you do to give him a beautiful weekend?" "In return, you get "beautiful yellow roses?" I told them to get their minds out of the gutter; "Jason sent me those roses because I accompanied him on a shopping spree for his new wardrobe." My co-workers followed me into my office, singing. "Here comes the bride."

The guys in the office also gathered around my office door. They had heard all the commotion and came to see what was going on. They saw me sitting at my desk, blushing with the bouquet of roses in front of me.

# Jason's Secret

One night, while we were on the couch, we were talking. Jason suddenly became extremely serious. I had never seen him this serious before. He was always happy and had a dry sense of humor. "Honey. There is something I need to tell you." he began. Concerned. I sat up on the couch.

"I do not know how to tell you this without just being direct," he said. "You need to know I am a heterosexual cross-dresser."

Being the naïve person I am. I said. "I do not understand what that means." He tried to explain as simply as he could. "Honey, it means I enjoy wearing women's clothes, makeup and shoes. I do not plan to have the surgery to become a woman. I am very fond of my boy parts."

I was shocked. I did not know what to say. Flippantly, I asked, "How old were you when you first discovered you had the desire to dress as a woman?"

"I can remember back when I was five years old, knowing I was different. I enjoyed playing with girly stuff while the other boys played with trucks and cars. When I was in middle school. I wore my mother's discarded pantyhose from her bathroom trash can in high school. I was experimenting with my mother's clothes and shoes when she was not home. By the time I was in college. I was sharing a room with another guy. I did not get dressed much except for wearing women's panties after graduation. I left home to start a new job in another state. I started purchasing women's clothes and shoes online. I did not dare to shop in department stores."

It appears it was a relief for him to disclose to me finally.

"From childhood, I always felt different from the other kids." he went on. "These feelings led me to believe I was a disappointment to my parents. I tried hard to please my mother more than my father. We lived on a farm, and I suffered from severe allergies which kept me indoors most of the time.

To make things worse. I did not have any friends. The only other person close to me was my mother. I found myself taking an interest in her activities. This developed my feminine behaviors, which were learning to cook, bake and sew."

I was stunned. Total disbelief at hearing everything he was saying. My mind was so overwhelmed. It felt like I was waking up from a bad nightmare. I jumped off the couch and moved as far away as I could. I started to feel repulsed, betrayed, and sick to my stomach. I wanted to hit him. I felt dirty and wanted to tell him to leave right now. There were so many thoughts racing through my mind.

I thought about my two young sons who loved him. How would they react if he were gone? How would our church family feel about this? Would our church ask us to leave and find another church home? How would our families feel after hearing this? I contemplated breaking off our relationship. I loved him for his heart and kindness and not for the way he dressed.

His voice seemed distant and very faint. "Noreen, please say something. I am so sorry. I did not mean to hurt you. I love you very much. You needed to know before we proceeded any further in our relationship."

Now, I am in tears and barely able to speak. I wanted it all to be a joke. A cruel joke but not true, at least. "Why didn't you tell me this when we met? Why did you wait till I fell in love with you, I wept?"

I could not tell you this earlier." he responded. "I had no idea where our relationship was headed. When I did. I tried several times but panicked when an opportunity came up. I was afraid of losing you. I wanted to be sure you loved me completely, too. I could not tell every girl I dated about my cross-dressing. I could not trust them to keep this a secret."

I had so many questions that needed answers. "Does this mean I will be labeled as a lesbian whenever we go out with you dressed as a woman? My attraction towards you is specific to you, not the entire gender. I did not choose this label. It is being forced upon me by you if I choose to remain in our relationship. "Yes, dear, we would be considered a lesbian couple," he replied.

I knew what I was hearing was not normal. It filled me with rage. I was mad at myself. Why didn't I pay more attention to the earlier signs of his characteristics being so feminine? Finally, I had to ask. "Are you gay?" He grunted. "No dear I am not gay?" "Do you dress as a woman to increase your sexual pleasure?" No, honey, this has nothing to do with sex.

I reflected on my own religious beliefs on traditional marriage and the meaning of love and intimacy after I recovered from the shock of his disclosure.

I realized how much I loved him. I felt sorry for him. I knew how difficult it must have been for him to keep such a secret. He had not been able to discuss this with his family or friends for all these years. I was still extremely angry. I asked him if I could see him dressed in women's lingerie. He agreed. We drove to his house, and he ushered me into his closet.

There were boxes of women's clothes and shoes he had purchased online in boxes all over his closet. He picked out the lingerie. He proceeded to the bathroom to change. When he was done changing, he walked back into his closet. "What do you think, honey?" Initially, I was so repulsed and suppressed the urge to throw up. I made fun of the way he looked. I was extremely mean to him.

Finally, after all this sank in. I arrived at a place of acceptance. I ultimately fully accepted him for who he was. I did not understand his need to be a cross-dresser(s) but decided to be receptive to his needs. However, I told him all the clothes and shoes must go. The clothes and shoes in the boxes were not what a regular female would wear. Maybe a hooker might wear them though I had my doubts. I began to question my own sexuality.

My past life experiences were an open book. This helped me minister to other women. They came to me for advice on domestic violence. I always shared with them my life experiences and my love for the Lord, who I have always felt was near me, especially through difficult times in my life. As a believer, I confidently wear the complete armor of Christ which shields and protects me from spiritual warfare.

Jason's major secret now became mine, too. This caused me fear, anxiety, and knots in my stomach. It made me physically ill whenever I was around friends and family. I could not speak to anyone about this skeleton that just came out of his closet. He came out of the closet to me and put me in the closet with him.

I did not realize how much his secret would affect my future life with him. How could I talk to my family about this? My only option was to isolate myself from my family and friends. I did this very gradually.

# Jason's Proposal

Our relationship and love for each other grew stronger over the years. One sunny afternoon in April. Jason invited me over to his home for lunch. He told me it was to meet his college roommate James and his wife, Sarah. Jason did not yet let James and Sarah know he was a cross-dresser. To my surprise, after lunch. Jason got down on one knee and proposed to me. "Noreen. I love you and would like nothing better than to share my life with you, will you marry me?"

Jason's cross-dressing overshadowed my excitement. However, I responded with love. "Yes, honey, I will marry you." We picked a date for our wedding which gave me only four months to prepare. I was quite nervous.

I could not help but compare Jason to my ex-husband. I realized there was no comparison. Jason was the gentlest soul I had ever met in my life. He was kind, caring, and loving to me and my boys. He did not drink alcohol, smoke or raise his voice at me or the boys. I sighed. This was the first time in my adult life I loved a man so deeply and completely. I was happy knowing he felt the same way about me and my kids.

He telephoned his parents to inform them of our upcoming marriage. He wanted to be sure they kept that date free. His parents lived out of town, and I had not yet met them. He had already met my family, and he seemed to like them. Jason's parents were also not aware he was a cross-dresser.

# Finding A Church

As part of the wedding preparations, we had to decide on a church we would like to be married in. Jason felt since I was Catholic, we ought to be married in my church. We made an appointment with my Parish priest to learn more about the church's requirements for marriage.

We patiently sat in the church office waiting for Father Jerry Jackson to see us. Father Jerry came out of the church office and greeted us. He led us to his private office and asked us to be seated. "So how can I help you?"

"Father. Jason and I are in love, and we would like to be married in the Catholic Church." I said. "What are the church's requirements?"

"Noreen since you are a divorcee. You will need to get an annulment. Jason, you are not Catholic. You will need to convert to Catholicism. An annulment takes at least two years to process. You and Noreen must wait two years before you can be married in the church. The cost for an annulment is a thousand dollars."

"Father. Jason is willing to become a Catholic." I said. "However. I cannot afford the cost of an annulment. I have just gotten through paying for my divorce. Is there any way the Church can help me with the annulment costs?"

"The Church can't help you with this as we have our own overhead and attorney costs, we must pay," said Father Jerry. I did not believe in the need for an annulment. I decided to keep an open mind.

"Father Jerry, could you please explain to us what an annulment means?" I asked. "I have some ideas. However, I want to be sure my understanding is correct." Father Jerry did his best to explain.

"An annulment is a legal procedure which cancels a marriage between a man and a woman. Annulling a marriage is as though it is completely erased— legally. It declares that the marriage never technically existed and was never valid. "Noreen, the reason for your annulment is that you were not spiritually married to your ex-husband."

"Father. I cannot use this reasoning. I knew exactly what was happening when I walked down the aisle with my ex-husband. I have given birth to two sons, which proves to me a marriage existed.

If our marriage did not exist, that would mean my sons would be born out of wedlock, right?" Father Jerry knew exactly what I was asking, but he refused to answer the question.

"You are not Catholic," he said, turning to Jason. "You should not receive communion in a Catholic Church. At the time of communion, you can go up with everybody else and place your right hand or both hands, forming an 'X' against your chest when you approach the priest.

This is a sign that you wish to receive a blessing rather than communion. Anybody is welcome to receive a blessing whether they are Catholics or not."

Jason pulled me aside. "Noreen, we cannot wait two years for an annulment to come through," he said. "We have two young boys at home. We do not want them to see us living together for two years without being married." I agreed with Jason. By this time, I was annoyed.

"Father. Jason is a member of the United Methodist Church. I am welcome to receive communion there. Unlike the Catholic Church they do not refuse any Christians from partaking in communion." I left our meeting with Father Jerry feeling disappointed.

In the car, I turned to Jason. "I would like to be married in the United Methodist Church, where you are a member. We can both receive communion, including the boys. This is important to me." Jason agreed. He hated to see me so discouraged and disappointed.

I called the United Methodist church the next morning and received an appointment to meet the Senior Pastor that afternoon. I was thrilled and called Jason at work.

"Honey, we have an appointment this afternoon to meet your Senior Pastor, could you leave work earlier a little earlier today so you can pick me up? I would prefer we take one car." "Consider it done," Jason responded.

I had never visited any other denominational churches before beside the Catholic Church. When we arrived at the Methodist Church one of the office staff ushered us into an office and asked to wait in there for the Senior Pastor. An attractive, casually dressed lady walked in.

We have an appointment with the Senior Pastor and were requested by your staff to wait in this office while we waited for him. If this is your office, we could always wait in the hallway." She immediately started to smile. I looked at Jason. He was grinning from ear to ear. I could tell he was struggling to keep a straight face without breaking out in laughter.

I thought to myself. "Am I missing something? I did not think I had said anything funny so why are they smiling? This must be a Methodist thing."

"My name is Noreen, and this is my finance, Jason. We are here to learn more about the church requirements for us to be married in the Methodist church. I am Catholic and extremely nervous. I have not been in a Methodist Church before. This is my first time."

I suddenly realized I had not given the lady an opportunity to speak. Smiling at me now she said, "I am the Senior Pastor. Your appointment is with me. I will be presiding over your marriage ceremony."

I was in shock, thinking "I am so unobservant. Why didn't I pay more attention to the pictures on the wall with the captions saying she was the Senior Pastor?" I realized now why she was smiling and why Jason was grinning. He knew she was the senior pastor and failed to tell me.

"This is quite different for me. In my church, only male priests performed wedding ceremonies." "Would you prefer a male pastor?" she responded. "I am comfortable with you performing the marriage ceremony," I said quickly.

We spent time talking and learning more about the church and the requirements needed for marriage in the Methodist Church. I was very impressed with the Senior Pastor's knowledge of the bible and her love for the Lord.

I now felt completely at ease. One of the requirements of the church was that we attend pre-marital classes which we did. After one of these classes, we selected the music to be sung at our marriage ceremony.

I asked a friend and coworker, Maureen, to be my Maid of Honor. For my bridesmaids, I chose my niece and my coworker Juliet. The flower girls. Jasmine and Diana were sisters and the same age as my sons. They were to be escorted by my two sons. Nine-year-old Joshua and Seven-year-old Jude. Jason picked his friend. Joe, to be his best man. The two groomsmen were his college roommate, James, and his brother.

My wedding bouquet and all the flower arrangements were gifts from a coworker and friend Juliet. I requested cream ribbons to adorn all her flower arrangements. Since this was my second marriage. I refused to wear white. I wore a cream wedding dress and veil. Jason wore a long-tailed cream tuxedo jacket with black tuxedo pants. This was Jason's first marriage. Therefore, I wanted him to be involved in every aspect of planning.

A month before the wedding the reception hall called me. They were confirming the date and time for the cake tasting.

"Would you like to go along with me for the cake tasting?" I asked Jason and was surprised at how happy he was to oblige, responding, "I would love to."

As soon as we arrived at the cake testing location, we were greeted by the banquet hall manager.

"We have put together samples of our most popular cakes for you to taste," he said. We tasted three or four samples by which time my taste buds were overwhelmed. I did not want to taste the remaining cake samples. Knowing it fully well, I would not be able to tell the difference between each sample.

"Honey. I would like you to select our wedding and groom's cakes." I told Jason. "Are you sure?" he asked. I nodded in agreement.

He quickly responded. "Would you like to taste my final selection before we seal the deal or forever hold your peace?"

I laughed. "I trust your selection." (I am not a big fan of cakes. He was most definitely a cake lover.) He finally picked the cakes and knew I would love them too. A decision was finally made after he tasted five more samples of cake.

He carefully selected the design and tasted the color and an intricate pattern for the icing on our cake. I was glad he made the decision. I was tired, cranky, and just wanted to go home.

I had a light bulb moment. Jason's mannerisms and behavior since I had met him started to make sense now. He wore my red printed apron in the kitchen at our potluck dinners.

He was too fussy in selecting the pattern and color of the icing on the cake. The comment at the restaurant when Oscar brought me a drink and the feminine way he used his fingers to put on and take off his eyeglasses. It has all become very clear now.

# The Wedding Day

Finally, the wedding day was here. Our families and friends arrived at the church. I began to get a little nervous. My bridesmaids were there to help me with whatever I needed. They reassured me things would be fine. I have a type-A personality and just could not relax.

I heard my mom's voice down the hallway leading to the bride's room as she got closer to the room. I heard her say. She is still my daughter. I need to give her my blessings before she walks down the aisle to be married.

I figured someone tried to keep her away prior to the ceremony. I was happy to see my mom and appreciated her blessings.

While I walked down the aisle, I saw my young boys, Joshua and Jude. I smiled to myself when I saw them in their little black tuxedos and Jason waiting for me by the senior pastor. The love I had for him poured out of my heart. I saw our friends from the singles group. They were smiling at me. Our friends were happy even though they were sad to see us leave the group. The music we selected for the service was beautifully sung by one of the church members.

The photographer was done taking pictures of the bridal party and our families. Jason, the boys and I left the church for the reception hall. We packed ourselves into a red sports car with the top down. The boys piled in the back seat, which was spacious enough for them. I took the passenger seat, and Jason did the driving. My wedding veil was very long and kept flying all over the place. It hit Jason in the face several times, obstructing his view of the road ahead. Other cars passed us honking and waving at us.

While driving to the reception Jason looked over at me. Joe Michaels called me early this morning laughing. He wanted to know how I was holding up the morning of my wedding.' 'How do you think I am holding up man? I am extremely nervous?' Joe hung up the phone, and before I knew it, he and James were at the front door ringing the doorbell. Joe said. 'We have the perfect remedy for your nervousness.' The three of us piled into James' car.

We drove to a nearby bar. Joe knew the bartender. He was one of his friends. He told him, 'My friend here is getting married in a couple of hours." Please give him a strong drink to get rid of his nervousness. Not too strong causing him to get smashed and out of control. His wife-to-be is also a friend of mine. She will never forgive me.'"

"We left the bar and headed straight for the church." Jason went on with his story. "When you saw me standing by the pastor. I was not only a bit tipsy. I was partially blind from wearing only one contact. I was running late this morning. I gave up trying to get the second contact in."

"I'm never surprised by what those two come up with." I laughed. "I am surprised how easy it was for them to talk you into going to a bar at 10:00 am. You never drink alcohol." "I needed something to calm my nerves and the alcohol did it."

Now grinning he continued with his story. "Just before we entered the church. James filled my pockets with marbles. They were weighing me down. This could explain why I seemed to be off balance to you." "Why did he give you marbles?" I asked. "He figured I had lost my marbles for getting married." Jason laughed.

# Reception Hall

When the bridal party arrived at the reception hall, my older brother told me the DJ had not yet arrived. He did his best to keep the guests entertained. Judging from the comments received from our guests, he did an excellent job. I felt a little sorry for him as he was close to using up all his good jokes.

After some tense moments, the DJ finally arrived. The families were excited; he was finally there. The families' relief was not even close to the bride's; I was extremely relieved.

The DJ apologized for his delay, saying his car broke down on the way to the reception hall. Fairly quickly with some help. The DJ had his equipment set up. The party began with food and dancing.

It was now time for us to leave the reception hall. We said goodbyes to our families and guests. We were led out through an archway of hands formed by our guests.

We were showered with rice as we made our way through the archway. I was relieved my boys were staying with Jason's parents in our home while we were gone.

We had not eaten any food at the reception except for sharing a piece of our wedding cake. It did not occur to us to pack some food from the reception for the night at the hotel. At 1:00 am, I started to get hungry.

"Honey. I am so hungry I have not eaten all day." Jason, being a loving and thoughtful husband, immediately responded with "Let's get dressed and go to a restaurant that serves breakfast 24/7."

We got dressed and off we went to get something to eat. We laughed all the way to the restaurant and back.

# Family Life

I knew Jason would make a great dad because of his nurturing nature. He had a tender heart and compassion for my boys. He quickly adapted to his new role as a parent. He took his parental responsibilities seriously.

The boys asked him. "Do we need to change our last name to take your last name?"

He responded. "You already have a dad. You do not need to take my last name. I do not need you taking my last name to prove you are my kids; you already are." What should we call you?" He replied. "You can call me Jason."

Jason's parents lived in a very small country town in another state. They were extremely kind to their new family and asked the boys to call them Grandma and Grandpa. The boys were excited to have young grandparents they could do things with. Grandma always planned fun activities she knew the boys would enjoy on family vacations to see them. Grandma baked chocolate chip cookies for the boys, and they loved them. Grandpa took the blades off his tractor. He had the boys take turns sitting in front with him riding on the tractor. This was the highlight of their vacation with their grandparents.

We made the decision not to tell our young sons about Jason's cross-dressing. We felt this may only confuse them and we could not take that risk. His parents were also unaware of his cross-dressing. We continued our married life as if everything was okay. Jason's crossdressing always overshadowed any excitement I felt in our marriage.

Our lives revolved around Jude and Joshua's activities, sports, church youth programs and social events. Jason was not a fan of sports or the outdoors. He suffered from severe allergies. He did not let this stop him from attending the boy's baseball and football practices and games. He made sure to take plenty of allergy medication before he left home.

While we were at one of Joshua's football games, there was a sudden, unexpected downpour of rain. Jason did not like being in the rain. He grabbed the towel off the top of the ice cooler. Put it over his head and held it away from his face. He did not want his eyeglasses to get water on them. I looked at him and laughed. At dinner, Joshua and I talked about the game and how he felt their team performed. "Joshua, did you see Jason from the field when it started raining?"

Joshua gave me a big grin. "Yep, Mom, how could I miss him? He had a bright pink towel over his head keeping the rain off his face. It was hard not to miss. We started laughing.

"Quit picking on me," Jason said. "At least I did not get my hair and eyeglasses wet. I cannot say the same to your mom. I was the one stuck later drying out her eyeglasses."

Jason helped the boys with their homework. They asked for help only when they struggled to complete an assignment. He walked them through the problems and let them figure out the answers. This frustrated Jude as he always asked for help close to bedtime. He was already sleepy, and tired and cried because Jason would not give him the answers to the homework questions.

Jason was not going to solve Jude's homework problems for him. He did not care if Jude cried. He was not going to let it bother him. Jude's emotional state did wear me down. I would whisper in Jason's ear to give Jude the answers so he could go to bed. I knew Jason was right. Jude knew exactly how to turn on those tears and make his mom feel sorry for him. This ended up in an argument between Jason and me. This started to cause a rift in our marriage. Joshua was in honor roll classes. He did not need Jason's help very often.

Jason took time off work to attend every parent-teacher conference with me, which also included taking Jude and Joshua to their doctor appointments.

I thought I was fine with him disciplining the boys. One night after football practice, Jason brought home his very angry twelve-year-old son Joshua. Jason got on Joshua's case about his bad sportsmanship behavior on the football field at practice. Whenever Joshua was mad at Jason, he took it out on me, and this day was no exception.

I was sitting in the living room sorting dirty laundry when they came home. Joshua walked into the living room mad. He picked up a stack of dirty laundry and threw it at me, hitting me in the face. Jason did not tolerate Joshua or Jude disrespecting me.

"I will not have you disrespecting your mother and my wife like you just did," Jason said. "I am going to lay you across my knees and spank you. You pick the day and time when you would like this to happen." Joshua, now in tears and extremely angry, said. "Let's go ahead and get it over with right now."

Jason was sitting by me on the couch in our living room where I was still sorting dirty laundry. He had Joshua lay across his knees and spank him twice. It broke my heart, and the tears kept rolling down my cheeks. I hid my face from Joshua so he would not see me crying.

Jason was very fair with the boys regarding the house rules. He first explained the rules and then the consequences. When they broke the rules, he disciplined them.

Joshua came home mad at me. He was stopped by a police officer as the tags on my car were expired. He did not get a ticket when he explained it was his mom's car. He was given a warning to have his mom take care of this. While walking up the stairs to his bedroom, he threw the car keys at me. He was now sixteen years old. He raised his voice at me, "I am not driving anymore. Here are your car keys. Keep them."

Jason, who was in the kitchen, heard the yelling and asked Joshua to come down from his bedroom. He smacked Joshua right across his face. "Joshua, I have told you before do not disrespect your mother. Pick up the car keys and put them where they belong. Now apologize to your mother." Joshua said he was sorry, and we all continued with the rest of our day. This was the second time Jason had to discipline Joshua, and we had no disciplinary problems again.

Over the years our sons grew extremely close to Jason and felt comfortable calling him "dad."

# Jason's Childhood

We lived in a suburban home located on the north side of Dallas. The boys attended schools with an excellent academic reputation. Jason felt it was important to live in the same neighborhood until the boys were through high school. This would allow them to keep the same friends growing up.

An opportunity he was never given.

When he was very young his dad worked for a company that required him to move every two years. Jason's dad was a hardworking plant manager. This had a profound effect on young Jason. He had to give up on his friends every time they moved.

"I wish my parents had discussed the move with me prior to it actually happening," he says. "It would have been nice if they asked me how I felt about moving. This was a painful experience for me. I thought, "What's the point of making friends?" I will have to leave them behind when we move again."

At this point little Jason gave up trying to make friends. He pretty much kept his feelings to himself at home. He had no childhood friends or stories to share as an adult. In Louisiana he made friends with a kid who lived in their neighborhood. The kid came over often to ask if Jason could play outside. He and the kid became good friends. His parents had no idea moving so often affected him so deeply.

His parents finally decided to move back to their hometown. They both had aging parents at home. Jason had to leave the only friend he made and move with his parents. Once the move was made, he pretty much kept to himself. This resulted in him not being able to make friends as an adult easily. He did not learn the social skills needed to make friends when he was younger and as an adult.

# Latchkey Kids

Whenever I traveled on business, Joshua managed to get himself in trouble at school. At the age of ten he spent a lot of time in the principal's office. I knew my son was crying out for my attention.

Joshua and Jude were latchkey kids. We lived in a new neighborhood. The school the kids attended was close to our home.

The School District Superintendent and the other powers decided not to provide a school bus for our neighborhood kids. It was also decided the school did not need a crossing guard to escort kids across the street.

The kids in our neighborhood had to cross a very busy street to get to the opposite side. When they got there, it was an easy walk on paved concrete to the school.

In the mornings on my way to work, I would drop the boys off at school. When school was out, they walked home together. I insisted they call me as soon as they got into the house. Joshua faithfully called. There were a couple of times he forgot to call. I called them and was so relieved to hear they were okay.

Joshua was a very responsible ten-year-old. He loved his little brother. Without hesitation, he agreed to take on the responsibility of watching over his eight-year-old little brother. He did everything he could to make sure his brother made it home and he made it home safe.

Joshua and Jude decided one day they wanted to ride their bicycles to school and back. I was hesitant. Jude had not been riding his bike for as long as Joshua had. Jude kept pleading with me, so I decided to give in and let him ride with Joshua.

Jude, who did not have enough experience riding his bike, was at first stressed because he was so slow and could not keep up with Joshua. He blamed his brother for deliberately leaving him behind.

Joshua, on the other hand, suffered from anxiety and stress. The added responsibility of taking care of his little brother increased his stress level. Considering he himself was a kid. Coming into a large two-story home with no parents to greet them must have been terrifying for him.

The School Principal called me several times at work. Parents were calling her office to complain Joshua was not waiting for his little brother to catch up with him. He drove off without first checking if his little brother was following him or not.

Joshua showed signs of built-up anxiety. Jude kept complaining about how Joshua would not wait for him. I was stressed, not knowing if my kids would make it home alive on the busy street. Jason was the only one who did not seem concerned. His family was stressed.

Joshua asked me constantly why I could not be like the other mothers and wait in the carpool lane for them when they got out of school.

With the constant stress of wondering if Joshua and Jude would make it home safe, I decided to quit my job and stay home with the boys. Jason and I discussed this prior to my quitting. I spent fifteen years with the company. I rarely travelled on business; however, when I did, Joshua managed to get himself in trouble in school and was sent to the principal's office.

Every morning, after dropping the kids off at school, I was home on my computer visiting job sites. I was looking for positions that allowed me the flexibility to work from home.

Since I was not contributing enough financially, this caused a burden on the family. Jason was resentful. I had more time to spend with the boys than he did. The loss of my income did not sit well with Jason. This caused another rift in our marriage. I felt the loss of my income too. This was something Jason failed to see. He seemed to have forgotten the reason I quit my job: "The boys were less stressed. They did not have to ride their cycles across a busy street without a crossing guard. Joshua was happy and excited every time he saw me in the carpool lane." Joshua's behavior improved significantly with me being home, and his visits to the principal finally ended.

One afternoon, I ran into my old girlfriend Sally unexpectedly at a store. I had not seen Sally in years, and we were both excited to see each other again. We decided to be spontaneous and have lunch that day. When Jason got home that evening, I excitedly said, "Jason, I ran into my old girlfriend Sally. We decided to have lunch. After lunch, I picked the boys up from school and headed over to Sally's. The boys had no idea Sally had a pool and were excited when they saw the pool. They enjoyed playing in the pool with Sally's son. Sally and I sat by the pool catching up on old times."

Jason's response surprised me. "Must be nice, wish I had time to sit by the pool."

I remarked, "I thought we agreed I would quit my job and stay home. This would allow me more time with the boys. Joshua's behavior and attitude have remarkably improved. The boys are always excited to see me in the carpool lane when school is out." I was now looking at Jason. "Why have you been so hateful and resentful toward me lately?"

I already knew his answer to this question. Jason wanted to play the role of the wife in the family. I would never agree to this arrangement.

Every evening Jason came home from work complaining. "The job is boring. It does not challenge me at all."

I finally said, "Your complaining is stressing me out and making me sick. If you are unhappy with your job; start looking for another job before you quit this one."

One day, unexpectedly, Jason received a call from a job placement company. The company's client had a position open for a Network Administrator. They asked Jason if he was open to an interview with their client. Jason immediately said, "Yes." At the interview, they made him an offer that was higher than what he was currently making. Jason accepted the offer.

This made it Jason's third job since we met. He worked at this company for one year before the constant complaints started again.

One evening Jason came home from work. I happily greeted him, "How was your day at work, Hon?"

Jason smiled. "At lunch, I put my feet on my desk and was taking a brief nap. My boss walked into the computer room along with his boss. I woke up but left my feet on the desk."

Horrified, I said, "Jason, why did you not go to the break room? You do know they can fire you for this."

Jason said, "That would be great. They will not invite me to attend any more of their boring meetings. They are boring, and I fall asleep at them."

"Noreen, you worry and need to knock it off. You are always being negative towards me."

I now started to get frustrated and irritated with Jason. I was about to start a dialogue with him but decided against it. Any discussions we have had in the past ended up with Jason feeling he was right. The stress of listening to him complain all the time started to wear thin on my nerves. I craved financial security from a man. If I wanted financial security, Jason was not the man to give it to me.

I started working full-time at the age of fifteen. My sister and I saw our parents work so hard to make ends meet. Their financial struggles only increased as all six children grew older. Our mom gave us her permission to work at a young age.

She probably felt since my sister and I were girls we would end up marrying men who could support us. That thought backfired. English-speaking women who worked in offices as secretaries earned a much higher income than their fathers or brothers with a four-year college degree dependent on the companies who hired them.

Most of the successful women secretaries were those who attended courses at Institutes teaching speed typing and Pitman shorthand.

The financial and economic conditions I experienced at a very young age cemented a concrete path tucked away in my brain. This path led me to believe it was my responsibility to keep a job earning an income no matter what bosses or coworkers threw at me.

It did not even seem to matter anymore even if my husband was lazy, could not keep a job or refused to look for one seriously. I was in constant survival mode. It was my responsibility to take care of Joshua and Jude as long as they were young and could not fend for themselves. This became the fuel that kept me fired up. I was quite aware of Jason's shortcomings. I had my own to contend with too. This was one of the reasons I became an 'Enabler.' I did not do this consciously.

I have now started to work for another company as an account executive. I worked from home. This week I traveled out of town for a company sales meeting. I was surprised when my phone rang early one morning.

It was Jason. We usually spoke to each other at night. Knowing something was wrong, I became concerned. "Where are you at?" I asked him. "I'm at home," he responded. "Did the company let you go?"

Yes, they did." he said. I laughed hysterically. It did not take the company even a week to end his contract. He mistook my laughing as I was okay about him being fired. "I am glad you are taking it so well." he continued. I had a hard time making this phone call to you. Thank you for making it easy on me." This was Jason's 6th job.

Dealing with Jason and his lack of motivation and desire to keep a job to support his family had become frustrating. I was forced to keep working to make sure some of the bills were being paid. If I solely depended on Jason for financial security. It would never happen.

I kept making excuses for Jason to his parents and friends. His lack of interest in following up on the job leads they provided him. I would constantly tell his parents and friends he was suffering from depression. He may have very well been. He was a grown man and should have been able to take care of himself.

Jason was out of work again this time for almost a year. His obsession with cross-dressing during this time only increased as he had too much idle time on his hands.

He had applied for a job with a government contractor. He received a call for an interview. After the interview he was called back with a job and salary offer. The salary range was $90K/year. This was the most Jason had ever seen in his career. We were both excited. This job would help us solve our debt issues over time.

The company hired Jason and five other Systems Administrators. The projects they were hired to work on were delayed. The company decided to have the talent hired and in place until the delay was lifted. The six of them were told to read up on company information and other technical literature in the meantime.

After about two weeks, Jason was frustrated and angry at not having anything constructive to do. He was bored once again. He was annoyed that the company was paying them a salary to do nothing.

I begged him to be patient. I asked him to spend this time catching up on the new software and technology updates he so desperately needed. He became very angry and started throwing accusations at me. He was now on his soapbox again. "You are never on my side, and you are always siding with the company."

I could feel myself tense up and anger building. I said. "I have never met anyone at this company either. I cannot understand where this is coming from. I have no clue why you keep throwing accusations at me. You are unable to keep a job for any length of time. I happen to have worked for many more years than you have. Therefore, I may know a thing or two about how human resources operate.

# The FBI At Our Home

I have some knowledge of what companies expect from their employees. I have been in the workforce for years longer than you have." Every job you have worked at has issues, you decide to quit, or they fire you. Have you given any thought to the possibility you are lazy, arrogant, and immature? He got more heated when I tried to explain to him what acceptable behavior was in the workplace and what was not. Unfortunately for our family he always went with unacceptable behavior. After this argument he did not complain anymore.

I had just taken a shower and put on my PJs as I was not feeling well. I decided to lie on my couch in the living room. I figured I would rest before picking the kids up from school. The front door opened, and I heard Jason's voice. I thought it was strange that he was at the front door. He always drove through the back alley using the driveway into our garage.

Then I heard his voice clearly saying, "Dear, I am not alone. There is someone with me." I sat up and saw a tall, skinny man in a trench coat walk in with him. He introduced himself as an FBI Special Agent. I looked at Jason trying to figure out what was going on. He did not respond to me and just had a blank look on his face.

The next thing I knew. A half dozen or more FBI agents were wearing FBI vests, walking into our home with guns drawn. I was stunned, "Please put your guns away. We do not allow guns in our home." They had some type of warrant in their hand to search our home. I just got a glimpse of it when they flashed it in my face.

I was asked to take a seat on a chair in our formal dining room. Jason had to sit across the table from me. I repeatedly asked him. "What have you done?" He refused to respond, which made my fear turn into anger. The FBI Special Agent with the trench coat started asking me questions about Jason. I was so confused my head was still reeling from them being there. The questions were directed only toward me. Jason just sat there stone-faced.

From where I was sitting. I could see the other agents headed upstairs. On the second floor was Jason's office and the boys' bedrooms. They came down the stairs with Jason's and each of the boys' computers. They also had files and disks belonging to Jason. I felt extremely violated as they went through each room in our home.

They were grasping at straws. Looking for anything that might incriminate Jason. At this point I was not sure who I was mad at Jason or the FBI. I felt so violated by the agents going through our personal stuff. Then a couple of agents who were in Jason's closet came out shaking their heads. They did not have to say a word to me. I knew they had found cross-dressing clothes. Makeup and shoes in his closet.

It was now several hours later since FBI agents invaded our home. I was no closer to finding out why they were there than I was when they arrived. My frustration started to show, and I became irritated with the FBI agents.

"I am going to my bedroom to put on some makeup and to change clothes. One of the female agents stood up and began to follow me to my own bedroom. She stood outside our bedroom leaving the door wide open so she could see me. I sarcastically asked her. "Are you going to stand there and watch me undress?" She nodded. "Yes, ma'am. I need to make sure you do not pull a gun on us." I responded. "You've got to be kidding me." It was quite humiliating for me as I did not change in front of any woman staring me down.

While getting dressed, I asked. "What did my husband do?" She did not give me an answer either. "My husband is a very honest man," I said. "He was once given fifty cents extra in change. He went back into the store and returned it to the clerk. I am not sure what you guys think you have on him. You have the wrong man."

I suddenly realized it was around 3:00 pm and the boys would be leaving school. I called my friend Sally. "Sally., Could you please pick up the boys from school and keep them at your house? I am not sure what time we will pick them up.

We have the FBI agents here with their guns drawn. I do not want the boys to come home and see this. It may be traumatic for them. I will tell you what is going on later when I pick the boys up from your home."

Of course, Sally agreed after about another hour or so. The agents collected a total of five of our computers and a bunch of files. They told us they were taking them to the FBI headquarters in Dallas. Once they were done with them, we would get them back.

Once they left. I immediately called an attorney to ask if Jason would be arrested. I suddenly realized I still did not know what Jason had done. I had him speak to the attorney. The attorney told us the most we can expect to happen is Jason would lose his job. Finally, Jason told me he was bored at work. He developed software that could crack any password. Such technology already existed, however. He decided to write one on his own.

He mentioned this to one of his co-workers, who he believed turned him in. I did not bother to say another word to him. I could not believe how someone could be so intelligent and gifted yet be so stupid.

We finally stopped by Sally's house to pick up the boys. We talked to them for some time and left with the boys to go home. The boys showered and went to bed. They had not noticed their computers were missing.

Jason had worked for the National Security Agency (NSA) in Maryland. He was flown to the FBI Agency in Washington for questioning. They threw a lot of questions at him all at once. They were trying to determine if he was a spy.

Apparently, Jason did not appreciate the attitude of the woman asking the questions. Therefore, he began to antagonize her, which made her upset. She had him take a lie detector test, which he failed. He thought the questions being asked for the lie detector test were stupid.

Once again. Jason exhibited his arrogance. He ended up losing his job just as our attorney had said. We also lost $6K we paid to the attorney as a retainer's fee. For at least two years later the FBI had our phones tapped, listening in on our conversations.

Five years later. We received our computers and files back. The computers were already obsolete by this time and were of no use to us. We ended up giving the computers away to single moms who could not afford a computer for their kids. Jason was kind enough to set up the computers for them in their homes.

The FBI episode caused a major rift in our marriage. I did not think our marriage could survive this. I was extremely upset and did not realize how disappointed I was in my marriage to Jason.

# Walking on Eggshells

I was walking on eggshells almost everywhere we went. Jason became so excited about his alternate life. I was afraid he would slip up and say something that would reveal our secret.

The financial stress. The FBI incident and cross-dressing had a huge impact on my health, which was declining fast. My friends jokingly said. "Noreen. Since you married Jason, you have always been sick. Are you sure you are not allergic to him?" I dwelled on what my friends said. Even though I knew they were only joking. I questioned if there was some truth to it.

I dismissed this thought right away. I thought to myself. "You all don't know him like I do." Very few husbands served their wives a cup of tea in bed. Jason had my pills sorted in my pill box for a month and called in my refills whenever my pills were running low. He prepared my tea in my favorite red aluminum teapot that I loved dearly.

"I am not sure what is happening to me. I have been sick throughout our marriage." I said flippantly. "It is probably related to stress. I cannot imagine what else it could be?" "Jason does all the cooking in our house as he does not eat Indian food which I cook for myself. As you know most of our friends in Texas love Indian food. The boys also do not eat Indian food and love Jason's cooking.

Jason is confident my illness is due to the change in my diet." "What is his point?" Shelia asked. "He feels it is probably the loaves of bread, pasta and starch he has introduced in my diet."

"I have become so dependent on him. There are times I cannot even stand on my own without his help. Very often, he must gently carry me off the couch and lay me on our bed."

The boys did their own laundry whenever they were home from school.

Jason did all our laundry at home. He disliked folding clothes and usually brought them to me to fold while I watched TV.

This did not bother me at all, as I loved the warmth of the clothes against my skin as I folded them. Any time I stepped into the kitchen. Jason gently led me out. We cashed in our retirement accounts to keep up with our monthly expenses. This time it took Jason almost two years to find his next job.

The new company offered him a decent salary with a one-year contract. His job was to automate the daily functions performed by employees. This allowed employees to use the time saved more efficiently on other functions needing attention. This is Jason's 7th job. I worked hard to earn an income so I could help with the finances.

"You need to start looking for your next job before this one will end," I suggested to Jason once again. Of course. He did not budge; he thought I was controlling every time I asked him to look for another job.

The company extended its contract for an additional six months. But it could not extend it any further. His contract ended. He did not seem to care. His family was suffering financially once again.

Almost every evening I came home from work only to find Jason asleep on the couch. It left me feeling frustrated. Angry and alone.

Every day I lifted Jason and our family up in prayer. I prayed, "Lord, this burden is too heavy for me to bear on my shoulders. I lift this burden up on your broad shoulders, Lord, to act according to your will."

The continuous loss of his income put our family way behind on our financial commitments. My frustration was displayed in anger toward Jason. I knew Jason was not actively looking for a job.

Jason. Still unemployed, I was absorbed by a company my brother and I established. From a technological aspect, he was a tremendous asset in growing our company. The company could not afford to pay him what he was worth. I begged him to look for another job. This was Jason's 8th job.

My brother also had a talk with him. "Man. we would love to have you. We just cannot afford to pay you what you are worth. Your family is financially suffering."

He refused to find another job. I sold my company shares to my partner and opted out of the business. He continued working for the company. Finally, the company had to let him go as sales were down.

# Joining A Church

We decided to join a church Jude frequented with his friend who had invited him to attend. We visited for several months. I loved the support we received from the church. Joshua tolerated the church's youth program. Keeping Jason's secret from our church friends was extremely difficult for me. Once again. Jason's inability to find work added to my stress level. The church members knew of our financial struggles. They had no idea Jason was a cross-dresser.

The pastor and deacons from the church knew of our difficulties. It was evident to them that he was not seriously looking for work. By this time, I lost all respect for him. A deacon from the church visited our home. He spoke to Jason.

"Why is it taking you so long to find another job?" he asked. "Are you seriously looking for a job? What kind of a job do you hope to get? Several people from the church have provided you with job leads. Why haven't you pursued these leads?"

"I am looking for a job that allows me to work from home," Jason responded. "I want to have my own schedule and not be tied down to a 9-5 job." "Everybody would like that too. Jason." the deacon responded. "You need to be willing to accept a job with any schedule. You have a family to support."

After two years of not working, Jason received a lead from a friend who was a member of the new church. "Our company is hiring, and I have referred you for one of the positions," he said. Jason was called for an interview and was hired by the company. This made it Jason's 9th job.

We praised and thanked the Lord for this blessing. We also prayed for our friend's family, who gave Jason the lead.

Jason worked there for 3 years when the company suffered a setback, and they had to lay off Jason and another lady from the department. The lady was not very technical, so she was helped and trained by Jason.

Jason told me the company started re-hiring employees that they laid off. I was excited and confident Jason would be re-hired.

My excitement lasted only a few minutes. Jason told me he, the lady, and another employee were exchanging chat messages. In the chat messages, they called their boss degrading names and made fun of him.

When Jason was laid off, his boss got the computer he used. He read all the chat messages Jason exchanged with the other two employees. Jason never deleted any files; however, the other employees did. When the boss read the messages, he told the other two employees he was debating on who to cut from the department, "After reading these messages." he said. "I know my decision to let him go was the right one."

I decided to join a women's bible study at church. Many of the women shared their joys and struggles. I just sat there and listened.

I could not come out openly and talk about Jason's crossdressing. I knew the pastor teaching our class would not be happy to hear he was a cross-dresser. I was not sure how the other women would feel if they knew this.

I decided to teach Sunday school for first and second graders. I had no idea why I chose these grades. I usually taught and mentored middle-aged girls who were 16 and 17. A couple in their late fifties began attending services at our church along with their nine foster children. Three of their kids were in my Sunday school class. One Sunday while I was in the middle of my study, one of the boys named Tim raised his hand. I stopped to hear what he had to say. "Miss Noreen, my dad is so strong and big, he beats up my mum and us every night when he is drunk." "His yelling is so loud, I must put my fingers in my ears to keep out the sound so I can fall asleep to wake up early for school the next day."

The other two siblings said, "Tim, mom said we should not speak about this." I said, "it is okay to let him speak." I turned to Tim and gave him a big hug and, "I understand how you feel and how scared you felt." "Tim's response to me was, how could you know or understand Miss Noreen? "Tim when I was your age I went through the exact same thing, I had to put my fingers in my ears to block the sound of the yelling too." Tim's eyes lit up, "you did." "Yes, I did."

"Tim, you said your dad was strong and big right? Is your dad bigger than God?" Tim said, "oh yes Miss Noreen he is." "Think again Tim, what have I been teaching you about God?" "Tim said, "you are right, God is bigger than my dad and I will start praying to God like you did. The kids are allowed to write to their parents and their parents can respond.

I did not have to wonder and wait to find out why I went through the trauma I did as a child. My experience connected me intimately with three little kids. Sometimes the suffering God allows us to go through is to be a comfort to someone else.

The parents of these kids will not be getting out of prison, nor will they get their children back. They are in a special program being raised by their foster parents. The foster parents have raised others in the same situations who have gone on to graduate from school, married and have their own children.

There were many days before I drove home crying as the isolation was gripping at my heart. I was afraid that if I told my friends they would ask me to leave him. My family would not want to hear or discuss this with me either.

We were members of the church for almost five years. I heard a rumor that the deacons of the church may ask him to leave. They felt he was not living up to his role as the head of the household.

He always argued with anybody who attempted to have a discussion with him on the subject. His response was always. "The bible doesn't say that only men need to work, nor does it say women shouldn't work."

I started to wonder if I was still in love with him. At this point, any love for Jason was quickly fading because I had no financial security. In church breakout groups, he always joined the women's groups as he related better to women than men.

This made it impossible for me to enjoy my time alone with women. He refused to accept the responsibility of being the spiritual head of the household or leadership of the family which I craved in a man all my life.

To spare him the embarrassment of the church asking him to leave. I decided to leave the church.

He did not know the real reason we were leaving. He agreed as he was not happy with the church. I knew by changing churches. I would lose my church family and friends I had grown to love there.

The real reason for leaving our church was because Jason started dropping hints about how certain men would look in short skirts and women's clothing. I was disgusted by this behavior and did not want to put myself or my sons through this. I could not even tell a person who I considered my best friend at the church what I was going through. Bible studies were the worst for me as I could not be open with the women so they could advise and pray for me through this journey.

It was with a sad heart that I said goodbye to my friends at the church I called home.

We had been visiting churches for several weeks prior to leaving our home church. We finally decided to join the Methodist Church, where we were married. The church had a large youth group.

The youth program offered several activities our boys enjoyed while visiting. Joshua and Jude loved the youth worship service held on Sunday nights.

We dropped the boys off at church on Sunday nights. Since we were already there, we decided to volunteer in the kitchen preparing and serving meals to the youth.

Since I was not currently working. I signed up for a women's bible study at the new church. The study was held in the morning on weekdays.

Jason and I joined a small group. The group met on Sunday mornings prior to the church service we attended. We were very happy with the new church and made several new friends. We loved our small group.

I decided to join the church choir. At church socials instead of hanging out with the circle of men Jason hung out with the women. I did not want to take part in the conversations with the women as he was always in our circle. Most women like to have 'girl time,' and I felt I could not since he spent time together with us women. There were times, I would nudge him, motioning him to join the men. I did realize with him being a cross-dresser, he had more in common with women. However, with him dressed in guy mode and the only man hanging out with the women's group at these socials, was embarrassing for me.

The stress of keeping Jason's secret was wearing thin on me. I missed church often as I was always ill. I had discovered that I suffered from Fibromyalgia. This is the result of overactive nerves. It is a condition that results in chronic widespread pain and tenderness all over the body.

Over the years, all the stress, pain, and anxiety left me physically ill every day. Jason knew I could not work outside the home anymore. The flare-ups and body aches grew worse as the months progressed due to the extreme stress my body had to endure with his constant chatter about cross-dressing.

I made friends easily in the Methodist Church. Our church group was very concerned about my health. They lifted me up in prayer whenever they didn't see me at church on Sunday mornings.

I was never relaxed nor at peace visiting anybody at the time. I wasn't sure what Jason would say next. He was getting bolder with his cross-dressing. I was afraid he would drop hints about his cross-dressing life. I continued to isolate myself from family and friends.

One Sunday after service. I went looking for him. I found him talking to the guys in charge of the music and cameras.

He was joking with one of them when I found him as I got closer. I could hear him say. "I bet you would look good in a mini skirt." The guy laughed and took it as a joke.

I felt my body get extremely cold and fear started to overcome me. He broke every agreement we set about his cross-dressing at socials we both attended. Situations like this only increased my anxiety attacks. I had to confront him. "Every time you speak to men about looking good in women's clothes it makes me extremely uncomfortable," I said. But he was no longer concerned about my feelings. "You've become so controlling. Get over it," he responded like he usually did lately. My symptoms got worse as time passed.

Today I was at my appointment with Dr. Brown. He has been my family physician for 25 years. I was led to his examination room to wait for him.

The fluorescent lights in the examination were too bright. I had a severe migraine in addition to the stress.

I turned the lights off and waited for Dr. Brown. I must have dozed off. Dr. Brown walked into the room and turned the light on.

"Please, doctor, can you leave the lights off? I have a severe migraine and the bright lights in the room hurt my eyes."

He responded rather firmly. "No, I need to examine you. With the lights off, I cannot do this well."

Noreen. Your illness is related to stress anxiety and severe migraines are the cause of the stress. I would like to know what's going on in your life to cause this amount of stress?"

I knew he was right. He saw right through me. I could not bring myself to tell Dr. Brown. "My stress is related to Jason being a cross-dresser.

Our financial situation is a disaster. Not being financially secure has caused my health to decline." What I didn't realize at the time was that Jason had already told him about his cross-dressing. Later, when I called Jason on this, as usual, he didn't seem concerned. "I had to tell him since my appointment was for an annual physical. He would see my nipples pierced with rings on them."

"Having your nipples pierced is a fetish and has nothing to do with crossdressing. Dr. Brown had been my doctor for 25 years before I even knew you. It would have been nice if you had discussed this with me first." "You worry too much. Get over it."

Jason rarely dressed as a woman during the boys' impressionable years. If he did it was restricted to our bedroom. I loved and supported Jason.

However, when it came to making love, the boundaries were set and made crystal clear to him. "I need to make love to my husband and not you dressed as a woman," I told him. "There will be no wigs and women's clothes during this time. "Honey. I respect your feelings, and I will honor them," he responded.

Over the years, Jason did not honor my feelings. He constantly tried manipulating me into agreeing to the bras, panties and high-heeled shoes in bed. This only added to the mountain of stress and pressure Jason had already inflicted on me.

Our sex life became non-existent over the years as seeing him become and act more female was a total turn-off for me. I had to constantly remind him of our agreement as if I were a mother reprimanding a child.

This type of manipulation continued throughout our marriage. Jason had become a master manipulator. He learned how to become one of the best manipulators from his mother. He always told me his mother always knew how to get her way with his father. She would first drop a hint of what she wanted. Gradually she would keep laying the foundation with smaller hints.

Before long, his father would agree to whatever she wanted, thinking he had come up with the plan all along. I continued living with this huge black cloud over my head. My friends, who knew me well, had no idea what I was going through. How do you tell someone my husband likes wearing women's underwear in bed?

# Un-Leashing The Beast

I was 6 years older than Jason. Cross-dressers between the ages of 40 through 50 cannot control their strong urge to remain in the closet. Jason as he got closer to his 50th birthday. His desire to wear women's clothing significantly increased.

It became difficult for him to keep his cross-dressing a secret. He sometimes slipped up in conversations with our friends. "Hey, why don't you join us for a barbeque hosted by our friends…stopping himself in mid-sentence. Realizing what he was about to do. Our cross-dresser friends were hosting the barbeque, and Jason was about to spill the beans.

The years had flown by so fast. Joshua and Jude had left home to attend universities. I felt Jason needed to find an appropriate outlet to express his feminine side. I wanted him to learn more about why he needed to cross-dress.

One day at dinner. I spoke to him. "You have put your feminine desires on the back burner for me and the kids all these years. I feel you need to find a group of heterosexual cross-dressers like yourself. This group could become a source of support for you in understanding your need to cross-dress."

He could not believe how supportive I was about him being a cross-dresser. He was so excited. He immediately got on the internet looking for groups in Dallas. Texas. I had no idea I had unleashed the beast in him. I felt he needed an outlet to express himself as a cross-dresser. I was tired of being fearful every time we went out. I had no idea I would live to regret this decision. If I knew my life would turn into a living nightmare. I would not have permitted Jason.

He finally found a group of heterosexual cross-dressers who were married to genetic women. He called the telephone number on the website and spoke to Rodney who was the president of the group.

He and Rodney communicated several times with each other through emails and phone calls before they met. They selected a date, time, and meeting place. Jason was filled with excitement and nervousness. I had not seen Jason this happy in a long time.

"I have set up a meeting date with Rodney and his wife, Destiny. Rodney suggested I bring you along as your support is very important. Rodney has a few more questions for us. Depending on our responses, he will give us more information. Rodney and Destiny are senior members of this group. What do you think? Will you go with me to meet them?"

"Jason, I had not planned on being involved with you or this group." "I wanted you to have the opportunity of being with men whom you could relate to as a cross-dresser." "But you have been extremely supportive of me as a cross-dresser. It would make me feel more comfortable if you came with me."

Jason, the way you have acted toward me and the disrespect you have shown in our marriage, I don't feel comfortable going with you. "Again, Jason whined and pleaded until I finally said. "Okay Jason, I will give it a try."

On the day of the meeting, he called Rodney to confirm the meeting was still on. We arrived at the meeting place earlier than expected. We waited for Rodney and Destiny to show up.

Rodney gave Jason a vague description of himself and Destiny. Every couple that passed by us wondered if this could be them. Finally, and on time, a mature aged couple approached us looking quite awkward. "Are you Noreen and Jason?" "Yes, Rodney, we are."

The introductions were made, and general courtesies were exchanged. Rodney asked Jason several specific questions relating to his cross-dressing. Rodney was satisfied with his response. He now gave us some more information about the group.

"Our group is very selective in picking our new members," said Rodney. "The places we meet are always kept private. This allows us to protect the identities of all our members. Some of our members are CEO's and Presidents of companies.

We also have doctors and surgeons attending our events. Therefore, we cannot afford to compromise their identities. If this happened, it would ruin their careers and most likely destroy their families. Listening to Rodney speak, I thought to myself, *"Goodness gracious, my life is going to change!"*

Jason was now signing the forms to become a member. He looked relaxed. Happy and content. While Jason was signing the papers, thoughts raced through my mind. Jason had no problem researching these groups on the internet. No problem making phone calls and following calls to Rodney.

In fact, he was in complete control of the process to become a member of this group. He was confident. Self-assured. Kind and relaxed. These were the qualities I first saw in Jason, which made me fall in love with him.

Then why did he have so much difficulty following up with potential job opportunities, Interviews, follow-ups, and job referral leads provided by friends and church members? To me, it became obvious he wanted me to work outside the home and didn't care if we were tanking financially.

All he wanted to do was paint his fingers and toenails. The forms were laid in front of me to sign. There were so many thoughts racing through my mind. The reality suddenly hit me. Smiling and giggling my thoughts were. *"WOW! We have just signed up to become members of the Cross-dressers Witness Protection Group."* I was careful not to share these strange thoughts with Jason. Any jokes I shared about cross-dressing, he would not think it was funny.

I enjoyed talking to Destiny who was very friendly. We shared our funny experiences married to cross-dressers. "You guys should attend our social this weekend," said Rodney. This will give you the opportunity to meet the other members of the group in a social setting." After meeting Rodney and Destiny. I took to them immediately.

"Where do we sign up to attend this event?" I asked. "We are so looking forward to meeting the rest of the group members. "Jason's jaw fell open, and he chuckled to himself. He couldn't believe how excited I was for us to meet couples like us. Jason was absolutely thrilled once we left the meeting.

When we were back in our car and headed home, he was excited. "I am finally going to meet men I can relate to. This makes me nervous and excited. You have such an outgoing personality you will make friends with the wives immediately." He hoped meeting wives in my situation would ease some of my stress.

At the meeting, Rodney had asked Jason to choose a feminine name. The other group members would use this name. This became especially important when attending group events. I had the option to change my name too, if I felt it was necessary to protect my identity.

I decided to stick with my own name. I had confessed to Rodney and Destiny that there were days when it was hard enough for me to remember my own name. "Can you imagine what my pea brain would do to me if I took on an additional name? I laughed?"

We left the meeting with Rodney and Destiny feeling welcomed. Happy yet tired. The meeting lasted the whole day, which was longer than I expected. The information provided by them was too much to retain and handle all at once. Once we got home, Jason immediately went to get his laptop. He placed it on the breakfast table and sat down in front of it.

The breakfast room overlooked the kitchen. He was on a mission to find the perfect feminine name to be used. He took a considerable amount of time online researching different female names.

In my thoughts I was resentfully thinking why had he not taken this much time and excitement in finding a new job earning a higher salary to cover our bills. I was in the kitchen preparing dinner. He began calling out names from a list he prepared.

Thank goodness he couldn't see me smiling with amusement. Being silly I remember thinking. "Am I having a baby girl, and nobody told me yet?" I could hear his voice in the background, sounding a tad bit irritated.

"I need you to pay attention to these names. Your opinion on these names is important to me." To be supportive. I offered my opinion on a few names he called out. Once again reality smacked me in the face. It was unbelievable. Here, I helped my husband pick his feminine name. He continued to call out more names.

Now, my patience was running extremely low, and I had reached the point of being aggravated. I was cranky, tired and hungry with a severe migraine. He kept interrupting me from preparing dinner by asking my opinion repeatedly. "I have already given you my opinion." Finally, I had enough.

"Why are you still calling out names to me?" It finally dawned on me. It was obvious he didn't seem to care. I had a severe migraine, and we haven't had dinner yet.

The only food I had consumed was something light for breakfast and a hot cup of tea. By this time, I was angry, "Good grief, Jason." "Just pick a name. How difficult could this be?" He looked at me in anger. "I am picking a feminine name which is important to me." I wish you would quit being so insensitive." Angry or not.

This was not the correct verbiage or tone of voice to use on me this late at night and not right now. I lost any sense of being compassionate. Nor did I care about keeping the peace anymore.

I have kept the peace for way too long. I wanted the boys to be raised in a peaceful home without their parents arguing all the time. Since the boys do not live with us anymore, it's time for Jason to hold his own.

Jason has done nothing but take advantage of me all these years. He was so confident I wouldn't leave him, so he kept piling it on thicker. I lost it and couldn't control my anger anymore. There was nothing left supporting the dam and it just burst.

"I have been very sensitive to your need to be a cross-dresser." "How about paying more attention to the name Jason." "The man I married. Do you even remember him?" "You have gone back to your old style of dressing before your transition to the new Jason," your closet consists of faded polo shirts and a couple of pairs of pants you wear every day."

'Your shoes are old and have holes in them, yet you continue to wear them, you rarely want to go out with me dressed in guy mode, and when we do go out, I am embarrassed by the way you dress as a man, you spend more money buying women's clothes than men's, when we are out shopping you head straight to the intimate section of the department store going through bras and panties, your closet consists of more women's clothes, "I go out and buy men's clothes, you may or may not wear, you have 20 pairs of women's shoe, 1pair of men's shoes.

"When we receive an invitation to an event not relating to crossdressing, you persistently ask me if you can go dressed as a woman. Knowing fully well my answer will be NO, the constant asking and pushing only irritates me. The more persistent you are, the greater my stress level reaches. We always end up in an argument which leaves me extremely frustrated and mentally drained. I feel like a mother reminding her child about our rules of cross-dressing."

Jason was shocked at my outburst, and I was too. Until today, he had no idea how strongly I felt about his cross-dressing. His cross-dressing consumed his life and some days, he forgot he had a family.

"Look. Jason. You have become very self-absorbed, self-centered, and selfish. You have not considered my feelings." Finally, Jason reason responded, "Honey, I am so sorry. You are right. This is a sensitive time for you. Please understand that your feelings are very important to me. I love you very much and will be more sensitive in the future."

"Jason, please spare me the I love you very much speech. Your feelings are important to me. FYI, Jason, this is not a sensitive time for me. Do not even underestimate my intelligence in believing my feelings are important to you. You are just manipulating words that mean nothing to you. However, you are yourself a passive-aggressive manipulator.

As if the outburst had never taken place, Jason said, "I have selected the name Faye Wilder. Honey, what is your opinion on this name?" I gave him the thumbs up and continued preparing dinner. I didn't even bother to turn back and look at him.

# Faye Wilder – The Other Woman

The other woman in our marriage was Jason's feminine side, Faye Wilder. Faye always hid her jewelry and makeup in places where I couldn't find them. I am not sure why she did this. Her complexion was very pale, and the jewelry she wore was not my style anyway.

My complexion was a lot darker than Faye's. It took her two hours to get dressed for an event. Once she was dressed, she ran around the house looking for her jewelry and makeup. It was very sad to watch Jason becoming more female than male.

I was gradually losing my husband to "the other woman." Faye. I had an anxiety attack when we were left home for a cross-dressing event, before leaving the house. I walked to the alley and looked to see if the coast was clear, no neighbors out. "I signaled Faye, who was running the car in the garage. She pulled the car out into our back driveway, and I jumped in, and we drove off. "Faye got irritated with me as I was afraid of the neighbors seeing us. "I do not care if our neighbors see me dressed as Faye. "In fact, I am hoping they see me so you can quit being so scared." I supported Faye in almost all her feminine changes. Faye didn't care if her secret was exposed to the neighbors.

I was scared that our neighbors would see Faye. I contemplated how I would respond to their questions. What would I say to them? How would I react if the subject of Faye came up? I felt there was no point expressing my feelings to Faye. She would get aggravated and tell me I was overreacting.

We were driving to the event. Faye gave me some points on how to address cross-dressers at our first social event. "When you speak to a cross-dresser, you always address the person as 'her' or 'she.' It is acceptable to address a cross-dresser in guy mode as 'he' or 'his.' When I am dressed as a woman you need to remember to call me Faye."

Going out shopping with Faye to pick an outfit for the event was very stressful. We received a few looks from people who recognized Faye as a man. Most people did not even pay any attention to us. I suggested a few age-appropriate outfits for Faye to consider. She had several reasons why she didn't want them. She was attracted to clothes that showed as much skin as she could get away with. She finally selected a revealing top, a short mini-skirt, and high-heeled shoes. This, of course, did not meet with my approval. I tried talking Faye into wearing something more modest. She didn't want to have that conversation with me.

I insisted she wear an age-appropriate outfit for the evening and reminded her Destiny at our first meeting said most of the members wore age-appropriate outfits. "You have a closet full of outfits, Faye. I am sure you can find something to wear."

Dealing with Faye on the night we were to attend the group event was absolutely maddening. She acted like a spoiled seventeen-year-old invading our closets, hogged the bathroom, requiring a lot of my attention and leaving me little time to get dressed for the evening.

I was disappointed Faye paid so much attention to getting dressed as a woman. As I had expected, Faye forgot where she hid her jewelry, she did such a great job of hiding it, but she couldn't remember where she hid it. This ended up in an argument. "I know you found my jewelry and makeup. You moved them to another place while cleaning the house." When she calmed down, she remembered where she hid them, and she apologized, "I am sorry for blaming you, I get nervous about meeting new people, I love you very much."

I was so tired of Faye's arguments and her ending them with an apology. "I love you very much, you do know that, right?" This happened so often I lost my patience and interest in going out with Faye. When we finally made it to the event. Rodney and Destiny were in the parking lot. They were getting stuff out of their car. When they were done, we walked along with them to the room reserved for this event.

As we entered the room, my initial reaction was shock. Seeing so many cross-dressers in one room was scary. Some of them were well put together, and others had room for improvement. You could tell very quickly the ones whose wives supported their cross-dressers and the ones who did not get the support. Their wives or significant others were usually absent or extremely uncomfortable at the events. Some of the cross-dressers could have used help with their makeup and outfits. This was our first time out in a group setting of this size. The event started with food and soft drinks. We mingled with the cross-dressers and their wives. Everybody was extremely friendly, which made us feel comfortable.

I had a hard time remembering to use "she" when speaking about another cross-dresser. My instincts were to say "he." By the end of the night, I was so confused I kept calling people "he" or "she." The group immediately took to me as I did to them. One of the cross-dressers jokingly corrected me when I said "his" instead of "her." They knew this was our first visit to the group.

They were just happy that I was there supporting my heterosexual cross-dresser spouse. I had several intense conversations with some of the cross-dressers at the event. It was surprising to see how much in common each of their journeys had been. "Growing up, we were not allowed to dress in female clothing openly."

"Therefore. It is not unusual for some of us in our mid-forties and fifties to wear clothing designed for teenagers. Unfortunately, some of the overweight cross-dressers also go this route. Our bodies are not designed to look graceful in these clothes. These cross-dressers negatively influence the image society has on the rest of us heterosexual cross-dressers.

I felt life should not be this complicated. The cross-dressers and gays spent years anticipating and planning their coming out. Whereas "genetic" women married to heterosexual cross-dressers or gay men in the closet, were not given the same opportunity. Also, society in general, including parents, siblings, friends and extended families are not prepared for their coming out. To them it feels like a death in the family. All their hopes and expectations for their children also died with their coming out. They need time to mourn the loss and grieve the loss of their children's spirituality.

Most cross-dressers come out of the closet between the ages of 40 to 60. They had suppressed their desire for years while raising kids and working to provide for their families. The few I met came from the computer and engineering fields. The social hour ended. Several of the cross-dressers started setting up chairs in a circle. They were preparing for the next session which was an open discussion with a psychologist.

Faye joined the cross-dressers sitting directly across from the group of wives and significant others. Faye sat like a guy with her legs spread apart leaving nothing to the imagination. This did not go unnoticed by one of the wives sitting by me. "Faye is sitting like a guy." She whispered in my ear, laughing. "I am going over to remind her to keep her legs together." "Go ahead, I smiled back." "I noticed this too when I sat down." She walked over to Faye. She whispered in her ear. "You are sitting like a guy; ladies keep their legs together, especially when wearing a skirt." Faye gave her an embarrassed look and quickly put her legs together.

The group meets once a month. Faye came out of the house closet only to move into a larger closet where she expressed herself as Faye. My stress was replaced with happiness after 10 years of marriage. I was able to be "ME." personality and all. I enjoyed attending the group events. The stress disappeared for one night a month. I did not have to hide the skeleton for this one night.

Like Faye I too felt excited. The skeleton I've carried for the past 10 years was finally out. I enjoyed speaking to women who had walked in my shoes for years. Every month I look forward to attending the events planned for the month. Looking at the cross-dressers. I could tell most of them took pride in their appearances before we discovered this group. Prior to joining this group, Jason and I usually dressed casually wherever we went out. I longed to dress in feminine clothes which I did for these events, of course it depended on how high-strung Faye was that night.

For this month's social we were going to meet at our usual place and then head to a restaurant. I was surprised to see about fifteen couples attending.

When we got to the parking lot of the restaurant, I saw a cross-dresser still sitting in her car. I remembered her from our first social. At the time, she was dressed in guy mode, and 'his' jokes were funny. He changed his feminine name twice. I wasn't sure what name she was going by now. The last time I heard she was going by the name of Michelle. I went over to her car.

"Hey, Michelle. What are you still doing sitting in your car? Come on out and walk with us to the restaurant."

I waited till she got out of her car. We started walking toward the entrance of the restaurant, talking to each other. I held her hand, remembering now that it was very cold. But I didn't think much of it.

We were busy talking as we walked together toward the entrance of the restaurant. Finally, in the restaurant. We were waiting to be seated.

"I want to thank you for being so friendly," said Michelle. "I don't think you noticed. But this is my first time out dressed as a woman. I was shaking with fear in my car when I got to the parking lot. If it wasn't for you being so friendly, ask me to get out of the car and hold my hand. I would never have gotten out of my car. I would have driven back home very disappointed."

"Really? I had no inclination." I said. "I am glad my talking puts you at ease. Usually, most of the time, people ask me to be quiet." We followed the hostess to our table. It seemed like all eyes were on us. I heard one male customer say, "Wow. I haven't seen this many tall women in my life. Where did they all come from?"

This statement made me smile. We were led to a very long table which accommodated us. The wait staff were extremely polite even though they knew some of the women were cross-dressers.

At home Faye wanted to be the wife. It was my responsibility to take on the husband's role, which I resented. I was pushed into the corner without a choice. He chose to live as a woman whereas I didn't make the choice to live as a man.

We continued going to the group events. We became good friends with several couples. At times, we visited each other outside a group setting. We met for dinner at a restaurant, or we stayed home playing cards until 2:00 am. The friendships I developed with these ladies meant a lot to me. They became our extended family. Faye's relationship with the other cross-dressers grew stronger.

The group organized a tea party once a year. All the cross-dressers and wives wore formal gowns with beautiful hats. It was quite a sight to see. We all glided around the room greeting each other. Several round tables were set up in the room. Each table was covered in white linen that reached the ground. On each table, there was a China teapot.

It was now time for the tea party to begin. We all picked a table to sit at. Once, we were all seated. A table captain was chosen for each table. The responsibility of the captain was to make sure the teapots were never empty. The captain poured hot tea in China cups for each guest sitting at the table. Delicious crumpets and scones were served by Destiny (Rodney's wife). She spent hours making the crumpets and scones. They were delicious.

The wives and significant others of the cross-dressers' group were very friendly. Making it easy to fit in. We sat together toward the back of the room whenever there was a guest speaker that night.

We talked about how our marriages or how our relationships have changed since cross-dressing. Several of the wives like me had come to terms with this. However, Some wives were still bitter. A few of the wives were still having difficulty dealing with their spouse's cross-dressing. The changes we experienced in our marriages were very similar. Wives who were bitter and angry found out after being married anywhere from five to thirty years. Even though it was hard on me at the time, I was grateful Jason told me before we were married.

There were still many problems in almost all our marriages. The major problem was often due to the cross-dresser's refusal to accept the limitations put on them by their wives. This ultimately resulted in several wives' refusal to support their cross-dresser's behavior anymore. The women who initially attempted to understand and cope with their cross-dresser lost their sympathetic attitude over time. I was told the longer a woman was in a relationship. The more negative her feelings were towards the cross-dresser.

Some of the women said their cross-dresser's behavior while cross-dressing was gentle, kind and helpful, making it easier to bear. There were others who, like me, reacted with initial anxiety and then support in the hope that he would "get over it."

This hope diminished over time and was replaced by resentment and anger. Every inch we gave to control or limit the cross-dressing resulted in a mile taken by the cross-dresser.

Most of us made the decision to put up with cross-dressing, provided it did not come to our neighborhood. We didn't want this to hurt our families. Friends and, most of all, our kids. Those were the conditions to maintain our marriages with the increase in cross-dressing. Sex in our marriages and relationships became non-existent. Those wives who disliked or were not interested in sexual activity were not bothered by this aspect of the marriage, for the women like me who still desired sex and were sexually active. The loss of this pleasure left a huge void in our lives.

# The Gay Neighborhood

I felt very safe going out with Faye for lunch or dinner in the gay neighborhood. We found a little Italian restaurant we frequented on the weekends. The restaurant hosted a drag show performed by professional drag queens. This was quite interesting and a lot of fun. We became friends with the owner of the restaurant. He treated us special as we were considered regulars. Faye and I would share a meal as we tried to keep our weight and budget down.

One night, the restaurant was completely booked so we stood in the hall area waiting for a table. The owner was clearing off a table for us. The owner sat us at a table by the window. The window overlooked a busy street of people walking around the gay neighborhood.

I noticed a nice-looking man standing outside the restaurant, looking in at us. Before I knew it, he was in the restaurant, walking toward our table. He sat at the adjacent table. Once seated, he pulled his chair closer to mine and began making casual conversation with me. The man's eyes were fixed on Faye and finally, he spoke to me, "Tell your friend to smile. She looks too reserved and needs to loosen up."

"Okay, I will pass that on to her." I smiled. I was trying hard to keep a straight face. I was hoping he would drop the subject of Faye soon. I was unable to warn Faye without him overhearing me. We were all sitting close to each other. Faye looked over at us and was curious about what we were talking about, but she didn't give it another thought. The guy spoke again to me, "Could you ask your friend if she would go out with me to dinner?"

Before I could respond, he went on, "On second thought, maybe, I should ask her out myself." It seemed like time stood still for a few minutes. I could feel my facial expression freeze. My anxiety took over and fear engulfed my entire body when he got up from his chair and headed toward Faye's chair. He stood in front of Faye. "You are a beautiful woman; would you like to go out with me to dinner?"

In horror. I couldn't believe what had just taken place right before my eyes. My heart was beating so fast I was sure this man could hear it. Faye, as calm as she could be, pulled me closer to her and responded, "You will need to ask my beautiful wife if it's okay with her."

The guy had no idea Faye was a cross-dresser(s) and looked shocked. He turned to me and apologized, "I'm so sorry. I didn't mean to disrespect you; this is my first visit to the gay neighborhood. I had no idea." I reassured him, "It is okay, no worries you did not know," I managed to reply softly. He was so embarrassed and was visibly shaken. I felt his pain and embarrassment as I, too, had gone through so much of this being married to Faye.

The guy left the restaurant in a hurry. I could not believe what just happened. I was always worried any time Faye went out alone. I was afraid if someone like this man at the restaurant approached Faye again, she might not be as lucky as she was today. We were later joined by our friends at the restaurant. We talked about this incident, but it was soon forgotten.

# Beautify Consultant

I was a part-time beauty consultant. I offered my services free to cross-dressers coming out for the first time. They had no idea how to use cosmetic products. I also helped those who needed to learn refinement techniques when applying their makeup.

I used my home on weekends to do makeovers. I asked the cross-dressers to bring their wigs along with them. I wanted to be sure the wigs suited their faces once the makeup was applied. Invariably I had to recommend a hair salon in Dallas where they could have their wigs trimmed in a style suitable for their faces.

I walked them through the application of their makeup, so they appeared more feminine. I was always very caring and sensitive to their feelings. I did not want people laughing or calling out cruel jokes when one of them was walking by a crowd of people. I disliked seeing cross-dressers wear bright-colored eye makeup like the kind teens and young adults wear. They had not learned how to apply eye makeup well and were often mistaken for drag queens.

This Saturday, there were three cross-dressers needing makeovers. I welcomed them into my home. Once everybody was seated with refreshments in hand, I started with. "I will be introducing you to several different products today. I will teach you how to use these products and techniques while applying them to your face. Remember, less is always best."

# Skeleton Revealed

We felt it was time to let our sons know about Jason's cross-dressing. Jason. It is important we sit down together when we speak to Joshua and Jude about your cross-dressing. Jason agreed.

Joshua, now twenty-one years old, was home from college for the holidays. When he walked in and greeted me, he looked around for Jason, "Mom, where's dad?"

"Your dad's at a meeting and should be home soon."

"Why are you not at the meeting too?" He asked.

"It is a meeting for men only," I replied. Joshua burst out laughing, "Mom, my dad is at a cross-dresser's meeting, isn't he?" His question took me completely by surprise. I had never intentionally lied to my sons before. We always discussed issues openly and fairly with each other. I began laughing too, "Yes honey, your dad is at a cross-dresser's meeting."

Joshua, still unable to control his laughter, yelled out, "I knew it! I knew it! "My dad is a cross-dresser, right, mom?" Joshua heard me the first time however, it seemed he needed reassurance from me again, "yes, Joshua, your dad is a cross-dresser. How did you find out?" "I saw the cross-dressers in our kitchen when I was home from school on the weekend. You were applying makeup on their faces. I suspected Dad may be one, too." "What are your thoughts on this?"

"I am okay with it, Mom he doesn't drink nor is he physically abusive to you or to us. He has always treated you well. That says a lot about him."

I smiled and hugged my son. I felt blessed that Joshua took the news well. He had no negative feelings towards his dad. I knew he loved his dad very much. Since Joshua already knew about Jason. I had to tell Jude too. Jude came home shortly after Joshua. Jude, who was now nineteen, was in the kitchen getting himself a drink.

I sat on the stairs leading to Jude's bedroom. I called out to Jude. "Honey. There is something we need to talk about." Jude sounded guilty. "Mom, does this have anything to do with my messy room?" "No, it doesn't." "Great." Jude joined me on the stairs. "Okay, what's up Mom?"

"Jude, your dad is at a men's meeting and should be home fairly soon." I waited for a response from Jude but did not get one. "All the men at this meeting are heterosexual cross-dressers." "Does this mean our dad is a cross-dresser too?" "Yes, Jude you are correct. Joshua found out earlier today about dad being a cross-dresser."

Jude, too, laughed, "Mom, at the age of seven, I saw large-size women's shoes in Dad's closet. I knew they were not yours as you have very small feet. Since then, I have always wondered about those large-size shoes. I now get it." (I remembered telling Jason when the kids were young to put a lock on his closet as I did not want the kids to see his shoes or girly clothes. He never thought it was necessary since the kids' bedrooms were upstairs). Jason, who thought he was smarter than me, never paid any attention to the rules I wanted to implement to restrict his cross-dressing. Jason never wanted to do anything in our home to hide the fact he was a cross-dresser. He did not care how this would affect the boys' minds at such a young age.

Jude suddenly spoke up and said, "Mom, you know Dad cannot help how he feels." he said, "his brain is wired differently from other men." Jude was majoring in psychology and had a sweet, soft and kind heart like his brother Joshua.

Later when Jason came home, I sat him down and said. "Jason the boys are aware you are a cross-dresser." He looked surprised and asked. "How do they know? Did you tell them? I thought we were supposed to speak to them together. What changed?" I briefed Jason on what transpired while he was away. "They have accepted you as a cross-dresser but most of all. They love you as their dad first. They have accepted it well." "It makes me happy they are so accepting of my new life change." "Jason. The boys love you very much."

That night at dinner. Jason talked to the boys. "Your mom tells me you know about my cross-dressing. Do you have any questions for me?" Joshua asked. "What do we call you when you are dressed as a female? Do we call you Dad?"

"No. You call me by my female name. Faye." The boys started to talk about college, and the conversation drifted in a different direction.

This disappointed Jason as he was ready to teach the boys in more detail about cross-dressing, however they were not interested.

# A Point of No Return

It had been two years since we joined the cross-dressing group when Faye decided she had outgrown this group. She felt it had become boring and could not care less about how much I enjoyed the people in the Heterosexual group.

Her desire was to venture out clubbing in the gayborhood. There was another group of cross-dressers who went out every weekend. They went bar hopping or visited other clubs in the gayborhood. Faye told me one night at dinner. "Let's join this new group. The ladies are very cool." I knew Faye had already made up her mind and did not care if I agreed or not.

"You want us to leave the heterosexual cross-dressers group to join a group that may not be all heterosexual cross-dressers, I asked in shock?" "Faye. I do not like the outfits some of these women wear. Their dresses are so tight and short. If they were to bend down, you would see their bottoms."

Faye used her passive manipulation to change my mind, and it always worked. I was mad at Faye for not considering my feelings. I did everything I could to keep my marriage from falling apart. I constantly remembered my wedding vows to Jason. This was one of the main reasons I supported Jason's new life as Faye.

I had made friends with the wives in the previous group. We had become very good friends. I was extremely sad to be leaving them. I felt once again I was leaving my friends behind. I would still see them, but not on a regular basis.

I felt Faye thought I was being supportive of her and kept pushing her luck too far. She counted on me being faithful in our marriage and felt confident I would never leave her.

Even in our social life with friends, churches, and cross-dresser groups, Faye changed these as fast as she did her employment with various companies. I missed all the friends I left behind in two churches and one heterosexual group.

I joined Faye several times for events planned on the weekends by this new group. Thelma. One of the cross-dressers said, "I wish my wife was supportive of my life as you are to Faye's." As the cross-dressers got to know me better. They enjoyed my company. Some of the new group members were rather creepy. Very few of them were still married, and most of them were divorced. Less than a handful of married couples were bar hopping with their cross-dressers.

Faye often went out to clubs with her new friends. She also started to wear dresses and skirts that were too short and tight for her. Faye was not concerned with my opinion on what she was wearing anymore.

Faye and Jason's personalities were completely the opposite. Faye was flirty. Self-centered. Selfish. Easily irritable and downright rude. She did not care if I was enjoying the night out or not.

She wanted to be the center of attention. Faye argued with me every night we went out together. Faye ignored me most of the night and was busy taking photographs when I looked at the photographs. There was only one of me.

Jason was very reserved, calm, caring and very attentive to me while we were out. He was gentle and very rarely raised his voice at me. Jason hated confrontation and would walk away from an argument rather than deal with it. This behavior caused a lack of communication in our marriage.

He loved to hang out with me and the boys watching TV or just being around us. He loved his family. When we were out, he was constantly taking pictures of me. He knew I didn't like my pictures taken but did it anyway.

# Jason's Priorities

Jason was still unemployed, and it was a rough three years. This time he became very depressed. He slept most of the day on the couch and was always tired.

His parents kept telling me one of us needed to find a job. What was interesting to me was they never questioned their son why he wasn't doing everything he could to find a job to support his family.

With so much time on his hands he became more obsessive about Faye and cross-dressing. He got upset when he didn't have money to shop for clothing and accessories for Faye.

I felt he should concentrate more on finding a job like Jason, buy some decent work clothes for him and spend less on Faye.

Jason worked in a niche technology support market. The computer hardware and software systems he worked on were a dying industry. He refused to keep up with the current software programs used in companies nationwide.

He claimed he didn't like the new computer technology software. He absolutely refused to learn or work on it. This made him non-marketable to companies in the computer industry.

He didn't want to go back to school to update his skills in the computer technology field either. It had been years since he used his electrical engineering degree. Therefore, he did not have the current knowledge. Skills or experience to be hired as an engineer.

One day, Jason talked to me about becoming Cisco CCNA and CCNP Certified.

"If I train and receive these certifications. It would make me more marketable, and I would command a higher income. To get these certifications. I will need to purchase books that are not cheap. It will cost us around $300.00 or more per book.

Do you feel I should do this while looking for a job?"

"Absolutely. Go ahead and purchase the books you need."

As an after-thought I added. "Jason, don't you think it would make more sense to enroll in a school to complete these training sessions?

In the back of my mind, I knew Jason would slack off if he studied at home even though we didn't have the money. I agreed to the purchase of the books.

He purchased the books and began studying. Within less than an hour he dosed off. His naps would last at least an hour. He attempted studying when he was awake only to fall asleep again.

I usually relax in the evenings watching my favorite TV shows. He would join me yet complain to his mother he could not study because I had the TV on.

His mother began siding with him against me. Throughout our marriage thus far she was very objective and didn't take sides. This is what I love about her.

"Why don't you go to the public library to study if the TV is distracting you?" "Why do I need to study in a public library when I have a home?"

It was a losing battle with Jason. He was like a child lashing out. He didn't like himself anymore. I gave up reasoning with him. It was apparent he was just making excuses.

He had no intention of completing the courses. He knew what the results of this action would be. He didn't have the knowledge to take the test for his certifications. I was right like so many times before. Jason did not complete the courses. He didn't even give a thought about the money we just spent buying those books. Money put on a credit card adds to the already overloaded debt we now owe.

The books sat on a shelf collecting dust in our spare bedroom, he called his office. He continued to be unemployed. He passively manipulated me to get whatever he wanted. I didn't recognize the signs and mistakenly took it for love. He would cheerfully do almost everything for me.

I became extremely dependent on Jason, which left him in total control of my life. I continued to isolate myself from my family and friends. It didn't help any, I was sick most of the time.

The manipulative behavior started whenever I was upset with him for not seriously looking for a job. He always claimed he was on the computer all day sending out resumes.

I asked him if he had followed up on any to which his response was negative. He continued to lie to his parents and our friends, he was busy job hunting. Our friends were shocked that he had not found a job yet since he was so technically savvy.

He left his computer one day while out for lunch with a friend. I happened to glance at his screen looking for something on his desk. There were a series of text messages between him and his cross-dresser friend. He confessed to his friend in one of the texts he was not looking hard enough for a job.

These texts were the proof I needed. Here in black and white it proved Jason had been lying to me for all these years. This disclosure didn't help anyone, just me. Now I had no doubt in my mind he wasn't actively looking. The guilt I felt for not believing him disappeared.

Jason loved being home enjoying his fantasy world of dressing as Faye wearing makeup and high-heeled shoes. Why would he want to give this up by working in the real world?

We struggled to pay our monthly expenses. We cashed in all our retirement funds which we spent each month. Jason's parents were very kind and helped us out with paying our bills and expenses each month. This was a significant amount of money.

I worked on our budget and cut out almost half of our expenses. Jason refused to do a budget or look at what I had put together. Every month when our finances ran low, he called his mother asking her for help.

I spoke to Jason's mom. "Instead of giving him money every time he calls you need to say NO, he needs to hit rock bottom." Even though I knew it would drastically hurt our family.

Like me, without realizing it we were enabling Jason's lack of motivation to look and secure a job seriously. I was constantly making excuses to Jason's parents and friends for his lack of finding a job.

His cross-dressing only escalated from this point on. His conversations revolved around shopping for women's clothes or cross-dressing. I was always made to feel guilty for being angry. He had become an expert in passive-aggressive behavior. I prayed all the time and did whatever I could to save my marriage from destruction.

I insisted on having a conversation with Jason at least twice a week about his progress in researching companies and career job sites and looking at new job listings. Looking for new jobs listed.

The time he spent on his cross-dressing would enter the conversation too. He claimed my emotions were out of control. He was going to call my doctor and request an increase in my depression medication.

I had a bad track record of discontinuing my medication without consulting my doctor. This didn't make him very happy. Dr. Brown didn't know the real reason why I stopped my medications. We could not afford them anymore since we had no health insurance.

Jason went with me to every doctor's appointment. Dr. Brown felt since he was the spouse he would be a better judge of my daily behavior. When he claimed I had extensive mood swings. Dr. Brown increased my dosage which resulted in me becoming overly passive.

I quit questioning Jason's decisions even though I didn't agree with them. By this time, I was mentally and physically weak. I had no strength left in me to argue with him. Besides, what was the point? In his mind, he was always right.

Jason was a procrastinator. He put off doing things that required a decision to be made by him. He disliked speaking to people on the phone when it came to our bills or anything else.

He hated it so much that he would pay the late fees. He never questioned the overage charges added to the bill. He just paid for it.

It was usually too late when he handed me the bill or another incident requiring our attention. "Honey, can you contact these people about this bill/issue? I have not mustered up the courage to call them. It has sat on my desk for quite some time."

His mother justified this behavior by saying he got it from her. His dad would question if she had taken care of an issue. Only to find it still sitting at her desk with nothing done. He had to take over and make the phone call finally.

This did not sit well with me. It further fueled my anger knowing his mother was still holding on to the apron strings, refusing to cut them. If she had, maybe Jason would have learned to be a man and accept the responsibilities that came with that title.

Several cross-dressers I met over the years continued to have very close relationships with their mothers. This ended up causing them dependency on their mothers. Their wives who loved them picked up from there.

# A Matter of Trust

The only constant in my marriage was my prayers to the lord. I prayed for the healing of my mind. Body and soul. I couldn't blame the lord for my circumstances. I acted upon my own free will when I decided to marry Jason.

One day I woke up and the cloud in my head began to clear. In its place came clarity of mind and soul. It gave me the willpower to change my environment. I decided I was done with being overly medicated and passive. I had left the door open for him to take complete control of my life. It was now time for me to take control of my once-sane mind.

Every morning Jason brought me my medications with a cup of hot tea. I stopped taking the medications I knew were making me overly passive. I did this without his knowledge.

After a few weeks of doing this I was finally able to think clearly. I knew there had to be a reason for my illness to progress so rapidly over the years. Running blood or other tests was out of the question since finances and other circumstances didn't allow for this. I was determined to find out why I was sick the past few years.

One morning, before I was given my tea in bed, I got up and walked to the kitchen. Jason stood over the sink washing my favorite red teapot.

On the counter lay a bottle of bleach. He had just poured some bleach into my teapot. I startled Jason when I walked in. He didn't see me walk in the kitchen as his back was towards me.

I proceeded to confront him. "Jason. Why did you just pour bleach in my teapot?" He quickly composed himself. "This is the only way to get the tea stains out of your teapot and mug." I was shocked. "How long has this been going on?" I didn't get a response.

He continued. "I thoroughly rinse out the bleach several times in hot water. I double-check the teapot and mug to make sure there are no traces of bleach left."

"When I see no traces of bleach left. I proceed to boil the water to make your tea."

"Jason, STOP right now," I yelled. "You have known how allergic I am to the chemicals flowing through the faucet water. I have become deathly ill recently and I knew there was something off in the tea you were bringing me every morning to drink."

"Adding bleach to the existing chemicals from the faucet water is a dangerous combination for my system." "How can you tell if the bleach is completely rinsed off?" "I knew my tea tasted different. I couldn't figure out what it was."

"From now on, Jason. Please quit making me tea in the mornings." "Also, do not cook any meals for me and I will wash our cooking dishes in the dishwasher and use bleach only if needed."

I didn't trust Jason anymore. I threw away my favorite red teapot. It was hard to imagine this red tea pot once gave me so much joy and happiness. It ended up being used to bring destruction to my body. I purchased a new teapot and made my own hot tea in the mornings.

# Playing With Fire

Jason's parents had continued to pay our house mortgage and other bills faithfully, so we didn't lose our home. Without their help we could not afford our house payments anymore. Jason was only paying interest on the home.

I sat Jason down one day. "Jason, we cannot afford to keep this large home running on our own."

"The only way we are still living here is because of your parents' generosity." It is not fair for us to use their hard-earned retirement to fund our home."

"We need to sell the house and move to the gayborhood in Dallas, Texas."

It was hard for me to imagine we lived in our home for 14 years. Jason. "It's amazing at the time we had this house on contract. I had 3 homes in my name."

"As you know my home prior to marrying you was a 4-bedroom 2 bath in an established neighborhood."

"The proceeds from the sale of this house were used by me as a down payment on our current home (3$^{rd}$ home)."

"You decided to purchase your own home against my wishes. You were more concerned about the agent's feelings than saving us money."

"You ended up closing on your new home. This resulted in your house being used as a giant storage place."

"You felt your home would not be suitable for our family as the boys' bedrooms were too close to the master bedroom. You ended up selling the house for a loss."

"Here we are living in our 3$^{rd}$ home having a deep discussion about selling it to move to Dallas. Texas."

"Jason, every decision you have made so far has caused us to lose money. When are you going to wake up and smell the coffee?"

With Jason still unemployed. I was given the opportunity to open an upscale home décor resale store in the up-and-coming neighborhood of the Bishop Arts District in Dallas. Texas.

My resale store was in what used to be a garage of a tall apartment building. The garage was paved with red bricks, and it had such an appealing look to it.

There was a side door that opened into a short street which I used as the store entrance. I found an old piano and Jason's mom spray-painted it bright red. I found 2 extra-large blue ceramic flowerpots which stood 3 feet high. I set them on either side of the entrance. People who visited the store always remarked how eye-catching the red piano and blue ceramic vases were. They used that as a landmark to find my store.

The bishop arts district was popular for its unique gift shops. Upscale delicious restaurants. An Artist working on his/her canvas on the sidewalk was not an uncommon site.

Only the best fresh ground coffee. Homemade pastries. Pies and cakes. Pizza places and barbecues are served on paper to be eaten with your fingers. It was finger-licking good.

The layout of the stores looked like a quaint old western town.

We found an apartment in the Bishop Arts District. Jason's parents footed the bill for all our moving expenses from our suburban home to Dallas.

I opened my resale store and ran it for two years. Jason did a significant amount of construction work to get the store ready to open.

Our apartment sat across a narrow street from my store. My store was frequented by visitors from neighboring towns. Some came from up north and others from the deep south. The locals and tourists came to dine at the upscale restaurants and some at the not-so-upscale restaurants. The food was good at any place you visited for lunch or dinner.

The shoppers shopped for large art pieces painted by local artists. Also of interest were the unique one-of-a-kind handmade products.

Bishop Arts was very close to the gay neighborhoods. The actual gay bars and restaurants are on Cedar Springs in Dallas Texas. On weekend nights all the lights are left on, and music is blaring from loudspeakers coming from the bars. With all the bright lights on it seemed like it was day and not night.

An upscale designer in the Dallas Arts Design District gave me the consignment of some beautiful pieces of home décor. As soon as she brought them in, they were sold.

Jason knew living in the gay neighborhood would remove a significant amount of my stress. He felt I worried too much about his safety when Faye was out alone.

Joshua after he graduated from Texas Tech moved in with us until he found a job. He was a great help and strength in running the store.

Jason made sure to let Joshua know if he was going to stay with us, he needed to pay us rent. Joshua had no problem doing so.

Jason refused to help me in the store once Joshua started a new job.

Jason was still unemployed. He would rather stay in the apartment and sleep instead of helping me run the store.

He continued sending text messages to his cross-dresser friend who lived in Houston. His wife lived in Dallas and had no idea her husband was messing around on her. He was so concerned I would tell his wife what he was up to. Jason reassured him I wouldn't say a word to his wife.

The store was bringing in an income. It was not enough to cover our house expenses too. Giving up on Jason getting a real job I made the decision to close the store.

It seemed I always had to give something up or find a job because Jason was lazy and didn't want to work. He had no problem getting rent from our son Joshua who had just started his job. Our rent was due, and we didn't have the money to pay for it. We were two months behind on rent.

Jason called his mother once again for money to pay the rent. His mother finally said NO. This was the worst time for her to put her foot down as we had no way of getting the money to pay the rent.

For the first time in our marriage Jason was afraid. He had no idea how we were going to pay the rent. I immediately went to my jewelry box and took out all my 22-carat gold jewelry.

I decided to sell the jewelry so we could pay our rent. I made enough money on the sale of my jewelry to pay two months' rent as we were a month behind.

It broke my heart to sell my gold necklace with a cross. It was a gift from my godmother for my First Holy Communion. I was seven years old and still remember that day.

Every piece of jewelry I sold had a significant emotional value to me. I remember holding the first gold ring I purchased when I was 21 years old. I could feel myself starting to get emotional with tears about to roll down my cheeks. I fought back the tears and emotions even though my heart was breaking.

I tried my best not to dwell on these emotions. I told myself I had to do whatever it took to survive. I knew Jason was not capable of helping us financially or in any other way.

Jason asked me. "Did you sell the gold necklace with the cross on it from your godmother?" "Yes, I did. Why do you ask?" "Well, you gave it to me as a gift, you do remember, right?"

"Yes, I remember, and I can't believe you would bring this up at such a sensitive time for me."

"You have become the most shellfish and thoughtless person I know." "How many years has it been since you last held a job."

"How about all the other jewelry I was forced to sell so we could make our rent payment? Do you even care about how I feel?"

Communicating with Jason was like talking to a blank wall. It had become difficult for me to look at him.

Jason finally applied for a job in a department store. He was offered a part-time job. I was happy he was working. Any income he earned would help our finances. At the department store one of his responsibilities was pricing sale items. This included pricing items in the women's department.

He enjoyed this very much. He could look at women's clothing and imagine what they would look like on him. Now, people wouldn't look at him strangely or think he was weird. He had the perfect excuse he worked there. The first choice of clothing for most cross-dressers is experimenting with women's lingerie. One day, we were out shopping, and of course, he went straight to the lingerie department. He picked out a sexy piece of lingerie and brought it over to show me. I thought it was for me.

"Wow. Thank you, honey. It looks great and so thoughtful of you." My excitement lasted only for a few minutes before he said. "Honey, I didn't pick this out for you, it's for Faye." Quickly realizing what he had just said, as an afterthought. "Let's purchase one for you too."

I looked at the price tag and immediately said, "No. We do not have the money for one and definitely cannot afford two."

He was mad at me as I brought up the affordability factor again. He felt it always happened when it came to purchasing something for Faye. I had to remind him I wasn't buying one for myself either.

Jason introduced me to his female coworkers while we were at the store. Jane, one of the coworkers smiling, came up to me and said. "It is so nice to meet you. I am so pleased to know Jason is married. We all thought he was gay." "We know now he is not." Jason worked part-time at the retail store for two years.

One day, Jason was approached by a company whose client was looking for a computer specialist. If he were offered the job, he would be earning a decent income again. Once again, I felt a sense of hope. Our financial situation would improve. This job was ideal for him. He would be working from home. Something he had always wanted to do. Jason was offered the job and liked it as he reported to a woman. Jason's boss relied on his technical expertise often. He was thrilled as it made him feel needed. Things were now running well for us.

Then one day he said. "I disclosed to my boss I'm a cross-dresser. I am so sorry, honey. I should have talked to you first. I sent my boss a link to Faye's site. She wanted to see the pictures."

"If you knew you should have talked to me first, then why didn't you." I often overhear your conversations with other cross-dressers. "It's better to ask for forgiveness than it is to get permission."

"I told her I had a beautiful wife." She asked. "Do you have pictures of your wife?" I said. "No, my wife doesn't like her pictures taken . . . oh. Honey, I sent her a link to your Facebook page."

This made it the second time he revealed to a boss he was a cross-dresser(s) prior to my knowledge. The stress and frustration with him continued to grow. I couldn't believe he had sent his boss a link to my Facebook page. He had become a cross-dressing time bomb waiting to explode.

The income he was earning was more than what he had been making in quite a while. Yet the fear of losing his job didn't seem to concern him. I knew he was playing with fire. Eventually, our family would get burnt if he continued with this type of behavior. When I communicated my fears to him. He just brushed it off as no big deal.

# Faye's Birthday Celebration

Birthdays were very important to me. Our birthdays were usually celebrated as a family. This included Grandma and Grandpa who were his parents.

This year, Faye (Jason) decided to celebrate her birthday at a club with some of her new cross-dresser friends. I was extremely hurt. Faye had set this up before letting me know. I decided not to go. This didn't seem to bother her.

I was sad about not being with her on her birthday. I asked Joshua and Jude. "Do you want to go to the club where Dad is celebrating his birthday so we can be with him as a family?" They agreed quickly. The three of us drove to the club in Joshua's car.

When we arrived, there was no sign of Faye (Jason), so we asked her friends if they had seen her.

Each one listed a different area of the club she could possibly be at visiting her other friends.

We finally found her, and she was surprised to see us. She smiled at us, and there was no excitement on her face.

She introduced us to her friends. She chatted with us for a few minutes and then disappeared, leaving us with a group of strangely dressed people who looked scary to me.

I was annoyed at Faye since the boys, and I came to meet her. The least we could do was have dinner together. We talked to Faye's friends for about an hour without seeing Faye again.

We were tired and ready to go home. We once again looked for Faye but didn't see her.

Her friend suggested we look at the dance floor. We got to the dance floor. She was standing there all alone on the dance floor, waiting for an invitation to dance. She looked so pathetic and desperate waiting for a man to ask her to dance.

I finally went up to her and said. "We are tired and ready to go home." All she said was. "Good-bye."

I was very disappointed and hurt. We had taken the time to be there for her. She treated us like we were perfect strangers.

I knew Jason would never do something like this. The three of us left the club without saying a word to each other. By this time Faye was living her life as though she was single.

# The Manipulation Game

Faye stayed up late every night. She was sending messages to people on Facebook. She was also visiting strange websites.

Whenever I walked into the room, Faye minimized the computer screen. "Why did you minimize your screen when I walked in?"

She denied this. "You're crazy. I didn't do that."

"Faye, I'm not your mother. You have no reason to lie to me. I am not concerned about which websites you visit. Nor who you chat with. I'm more concerned about this activity and keeping you up till 3:00 am in the morning. You are a grouch the next day and difficult to live with. You are not getting enough sleep. You complain to your mother that I'm the cause of this. It is time for you to grow up and cut the apron strings."

I could not handle Faye lying to me. She was laying the foundation for a deadly game, and I was her target. This proved to be true when I read one of her text messages, which I printed between her and her friend.

Faye sent a text to her friend saying. "I think she's (me) on the phone with her oldest brother. Once she falls asleep, I will look at her call log to be sure that it is who it was. I need to call her oldest brother. He needs to be convinced she needs to be committed."

I confronted Faye. "I printed out the text messages between you and your friend. You are playing a sick game. Good luck convincing my family to have me committed. It is not going to happen, so don't even try it."

Through all the ups and downs of my marriage. I stayed faithful to Faye (Jason). I kept reminding myself of my wedding vows. I seriously felt my responsibility was to stand by my man no matter how bad things were. Mental abuse is so much more destructive than verbal and physical abuse. It was scary what Faye might do to me to get me out of the picture. She has tried several things. The good Lord protected me just in time.

# Faye's infidelity with Felicia

Almost all the heterosexual cross-dressers I met were very protective of their wife's or significant others' privacy. They usually left home at night wearing a disguise over their female clothing. They selected a suitable disguise to avoid exposing their identity to maintain their wife's or significant others' identities. They very rarely left home during the day.

Faye did not wear a disguise when she went out, nor did she restrict herself to going out only at night. I understood and was sensitive towards Faye's desire to be accepted as a woman. However, I resented her for compromising my and our sons' privacy by bringing herself into our neighborhood. Several people in the neighborhood who saw her knew it was Jason. They made fun of her behind her back.

Faye invited me to go bar hopping with her friends on the weekends. I refused the invitations as I was upset with her for coming out openly in our neighborhood. Faye went out every weekend with her friends. She put off going to visit her parents. Her cross-dress events were more important. If she visited her parents, she would have to go into guy mode dressed as Jason. Her parents were unaware of their son being a cross-dresser.

I noticed for a couple of weeks Faye seemed happier than she had been in a long time. She kept talking about a new cross-dresser friend she had just met named Felicia. Faye said. "You are probably tired of always hearing me talk about my new friend."

"That's fine with me," I replied. "I am happy to hear you communicate your feelings for your friend to me. You have always had a hard time expressing your feelings as you kept them to yourself. It has been a long time since we have communicated on such a deep level."

Faye went on to say. "Felicia has helped me overcome my insecurities and tells me how feminine and pretty I look."

I stopped her in her tracks. "Hold Up, I have been doing and saying the same things to you all these years. I have supported you as a cross-dresser(s) for fifteen years."

"Faye. You speak of this person like you used to me when we first met. Are you in love with this person?"

"Maybe or maybe not." With a smile on her face. "I'm definitely attracted to Felicia and have feelings for her."

"Please be patient with me while I get this all sorted out in my mind. Felicia does not feel the same way about me. This relationship is not going anywhere since Felicia is married too." "She has no intention of leaving her wife." "Why would she? Her wife is a psychologist." "Felicia has a job you don't."

"All Felicia wants from you is to continue following her around with your camera. Taking various posing shots of herself. She has found a free personal Photographer at her disposal. She doesn't have to pay you a single dime."

After a bit, Faye shocked me. "All Felicia and I did was exchange a kiss and that's all." "Do you realize what you are saying, Faye?" I was horrified. "Be patient with you while you sort out your feelings in your mind for this woman called Felicia."

"Have you completely lost your Christian values and morals? Do you even believe in Jesus Christ anymore?" "The devil is controlling you. Why else would you hand over your bible to me and not take it with you?"

"Don't you think you manipulated me long enough in giving you time to figure out if you wanted to live as Jason or Faye?" Knowing fully well you were already gay."

Faye tried to squirm her way out of this like the snake she was. Faye knew she had already said way too much. "Faye, do you realize you kissed a man?" "I kissed a woman named Felicia." Faye kept repeating this repeatedly. Finally, she stopped.

"I felt very uncomfortable when I kissed her. It felt like I was cheating on you." "Yes. Faye. You were cheating on me. The fact you had feelings for another person was enough to tell you this was not right."

"All you had to do was tell me and I would have arranged to get a divorce. I do not want to be with a person who isn't in love with me anymore.

"Instead, you chose to be a coward by drugging me. Wanting to convince my brother I needed to be committed. Doing everything possible to make me physically ill-using bleach in my mugs and teapots. Telling your parents how I was mistreating you."

"In fact, you made members of our previous churches believe I was dominating you. You used my personality of being loud and extremely outspoken to cement your case of a wife who did not give you an opportunity to speak."

"Even when the youth pastor of our first church told me, my husband should drag me by my hair to make sure I was obedient to you. I saw the shock on your face when you heard it. Yet, when I tried to verify it with you while he was still in our home. You denied hearing it. You couldn't even look me in the face. This was a result of me telling him he acted too liberal on a youth trip we had just returned from.

"Then again, you refused to speak up or come to my defense when your mother was blaming me for the problems we were having in our marriage." "In fact, you agreed with her." "I could have yelled back at your mother and told her exactly what was going on in our marriage." "I just didn't have the heart to hurt her."

"You were so afraid of your mother that you didn't have the guts to ask me for a divorce." "You had to set a web of lies to convince them I was the cause of the problems."

"When I thought things couldn't get any worse than they were, you blamed me for the reason you had an affair with Felicia. If you had only gone out with me on the weekends, this would never have happened.

I was so lonely without you. I fell into the arms of another woman for comfort."

"Jason, you know you are spitting out a bunch of bull crap. Give it a rest, my eyes are wide open, and I am not falling for your passive aggressive behavior."

"You should have set boundaries for me when I went out alone." "Firstly, you are a middle-aged married man and should not be out at bars at night acting as if you are single.

Secondly, "You are not a child; I shouldn't have to set boundaries for you. You are a grown man who knows right from wrong. Quit blaming me for your infidelity. You refuse to accept responsibility for your own actions."

"Honey, I still love you and will come home to you every night, I am not going anywhere else. I am not gay and still want to be with you."

"Jason, give it up. These are not your words, they are Felicia's. You are gay, and it is about time you admitted it to yourself. You came out of the closet as a cross-dresser. You should have come out as a gay man."

"You have ruined my life, my finances and your parent's finances. Quit trying to ruin another woman's life. Your mother, bless her heart, may have blinders on where you are considered. I don't anymore."

This discussion emotionally drained me. It took me weeks to get over Faye's infidelity. I loved Jason very much and did not want my marriage to end.

"I am going to meet Felicia for lunch," Faye told me. "Both of us will be dressed in guy mode. I want to find out if this attraction is even real." When Jason came back home from lunch, he seemed relieved.

"Everything is okay. I am not attracted to Felicia as a man at all." "What does this mean? Are you no longer attracted to Felicia, the feminine side?"

"My feelings for Felicia have not changed. I am still trying to sort these feelings out in my mind."

# Fetish and Bondage

Faye told me she was going to a club that Felicia and a group of other cross-dressers thought she might like. This was a club where people lived out their fantasies.

This club inflicted pain on each other for sexual pleasure with a willing partner. Felicia was no stranger to this club. Felicia told Faye to call her anytime she wanted to live out her fantasy. She would be Faye's willing partner.

I already knew Jason liked the fetishistic life. I was opposed to this type of sexual play. I had communicated this to Jason when he brought it up when we first met. Jason was very considerate of my feelings and did not push the issue with me.

Faye now began being very honest with me. She told me about Felicia volunteering to be her sexual play partner. Faye suggested I keep an open mind and go with her to check this new place out. When Faye told me what a sexual partner did. I quickly changed my mind.

"Faye. If anyone's going to inflict pain on you for your sexual pleasure, it will be me. Not Felicia." Besides, have you lost your mind? Why would you even think I would be okay with you having an intimate relationship with anyone?

We arrived at the place. I immediately started to tense up and get nervous; Faye told me she was nervous, too, as this was her first time in a place like this.

We were welcomed in and led to a large room. This room was where all the play took place. There were different types of play equipment laid out neatly for those who wanted to participate in the play. The ground rules were explained.

Once they were done explaining the rules. The fear set in, and I began to get afraid when I saw all the play equipment. There were several people already in the room engaged in play.

It was hard for me to believe this pain could be enjoyable. There were two huge wooden crosses mounted flush against one wall. On the other side of the room there were makeshift wooden beds. The beds consisted of planks of wood placed horizontally across. Supported and attached to wooden vertical support legs.

On one of the beds there was a woman tied up face down and her partner was spanking her with what looked like a flat lightweight paddle. There were also other objects that I did not stick around to see.

There was another woman who was screaming extremely loudly. It seemed like all the visitors moved closer toward the screams. We found a woman tied up off the floor in what looked like a cage made of ropes with large loops.

Her partner was under the rope cage, beating her bottom with what appeared to be a bat. The woman's bottom was filled with blisters that had turned blue. We were told she was screaming out of pleasure. She was enjoying this type of play. I told Faye I needed to move away as I couldn't bear to watch this anymore.

The woman on the bed who had been spanked eventually reached a state of sub-consciousness. Her partner carried her off the bed and cradled her on a couch to bring her gently back to consciousness. In this play the partner could have been a spouse, significant other, friend or a person she hired to spank her.

I was told by another lady in the room it was common for the play partners to share an intimate sexual relationship outside their marriages. The partners' relationship continued often without the wife or significant other's knowledge.

She said she too, was married and a play partner to another man. Her husband disliked it and was upset with what she was doing. However, she refused to stop.

I quickly realized this place was frequented by many of the married cross-dressers. Most of their wives or significant others had no idea their cross-dressers were engaged in this type of sexual pleasure. The ones that knew had no interest in going along, they preferred their cross-dressers to go and do their own thing. This would not be true in my case with Faye.

I knew that Faye was not capable of separating her feelings easily. She could very easily end up emotionally and physically involved with her sex partner.

She was truthful and honest with me when it came to her fantasies. She wanted me to inflict pain on her as it gave her a sexual release and satisfaction.

We were there for an hour and that was enough for me. I told Faye this was not what I wanted in my marriage, so we decided to leave.

Going forward, I could never trust Faye to be faithful in our marriage. I wouldn't trust her at all. This life was too exciting for her, and she wanted to experience it all. Even if it meant lying to me, she would have had no consciousness or regret.

In fact, Faye had already set up a session with Felicia, giving her permission to be her sexual partner without even consulting me. I was not prepared to get any type of sexual disease if she engaged in multiple partners.

Faye indicated she would prefer to have me as her partner. She felt this may enhance our marriage. Faye lost her fear of God, ran around as if she was single and spent money as if she was earning it.

The scene played out in this place was nothing more than a sick satanic play. I could not believe I allowed myself to be manipulated in the guise of saving my marriage into coming here by Faye.

# Visit to Ellen's Bar

Faye dropped me off at a local bar where her cross-dresser friends were gathering. She could not stay as she was on her way to a scheduled knot tying class. The plan was to have Faye join me once she was done. At night I met Teresa, a cross-dresser friend of ours. Teresa was in the process of transitioning to becoming a woman. She had financially planned to have the surgery done for quite some time. She looked sad and upset. "What's wrong? Teresa. You look so sad. Why are you crying? "My lover is a heterosexual cross-dresser(s) just like me. He is married to a genetic woman. He broke up our relationship to save his marriage. I feel so betrayed." I knew exactly who Teresa was talking about as well as his wife and kids.

Teresa took me totally by surprise when she asked. "Does Faye show any signs of gay tendencies?" I immediately said. "No." I hesitated for a few minutes. "Teresa, why did you ask me that question?" "Faye told me she has feelings for Felicia and said it was just a kiss. But I do not believe her, I feel it was more than that. Now I was crying. "Teresa. I do not understand Faye and Felicia's relationship." Honey, that girl has nothing over you. She is a tramp and a bimbo. Everybody in the gay community knows this about her.

"The temperature in the bar was getting stuffy so I proceeded to the patio to get some fresh air and wait on Faye. Sue had the same idea and when she saw me, she motioned me to sit by her. Sue's husband was the one who was having an affair with Teresa. I decided to take the seat. Sue immediately started talking about her husband's infidelity and blamed Teresa for their marital issues.

Sue proceeded to tell me about Abomination and how her bible study group, and the church congregation were praying for her. Sue said, "Noreen now that you know it is a sin, what are you going to do about it?" I looked at her in shock and said, "Sue, how could you even ask me that question? You have been a believer for way longer than I have been. Your bible study group and church congregation have been praying for you for years, and yet you remain married to your husband. Sue, I have decided to divorce Faye based on our conversation today.

Sue started to laugh, "Noreen, you are not weak, are you?" "not weak, too trusting but not anymore." Before I left Sue said, "Thank you Noreen." I looked back and winked at her smiling, "for what dear?" We both laughed as we realized we had put up with enough madness. The next part of our lives was going to be lived for God, ourselves and our kids.

Faye was done with her class and joined me at the club. It was late; therefore, we decided to head home and call it a night.

The next day Faye asked me, "what did you say to Sue last night? Her husband called me to let me know Sue filed for divorce. The last person he saw Sue speaking to last night was you." I responded, "maybe he should ask his wife and not you."

One night, Faye invited me to have dinner with Felicia and another couple to prove there was not anything between them. As we were getting out of the car. Faye pointed me in the direction of a woman walking toward the restaurant we were to meet at.

"That's Felicia walking down the street towards the restaurant." Faye looked very happy and excited. It was hard not to miss. When we were seated in the restaurant.

I got a better glimpse of Felicia's outfit. It was made of some sort of weird plastic fabric. The skirt flared out and under the skirt she had a stiff netting fabric holding it up.

The skirt was way too short. She wore long, lacey underwear which was very visible. It left nothing to the imagination. She knew her underwear was showing but didn't care. She loved the attention she was getting from the patrons at the restaurant, even though it was negative.

I did not recognize Jason anymore in our marriage. Faye had completely taken over and did whatever she pleased. She stopped letting me know where she was going or what time she was coming home. Weeks went by and Faye continued to chat with her friends. She continued to minimize the computer screen when I walked into the room.

There were times Faye left the house when she received a phone call. I would later see her in the car talking to somebody with the car doors locked. Seeing her being so secretive only increased my anxiety.

I started to get paranoid about Faye's behavior and was upset with her most of the time. I didn't trust her anymore. I knew she was lying to me often.

This behavior of Faye's continued. I was suffering from a broken heart. I didn't want her to know how much she truly hurt me with her affair with Felicia.

# Faye the Bar Hopper

Things changed in the last six months of our marriage. This was when Felicia showed up in our lives. Even though I knew in my heart, Faye's attraction to Felicia would fade away in time.

I was the first girl Jason had seriously dated. I knew he had not experienced the parties and fun I did as a teenager. Faye was living the life Jason had missed as a teenager. For the first time in her life, she was having fun. She bragged about making new friends on her own without my help. She looked forward to the weekends so she could party with her friends.

Faye came up with an agreement. This would allow Faye to be carefree with limitations. She could spend time with other cross-dressers provided things were handled appropriately.

I felt Faye was the other woman in Jason's life. He was very obsessed with his feminine side. I felt Jason's feelings for Faye were stronger than they were for me. His interest was in what Faye wanted to do rather than what I wanted to do.

While Faye was out one weekend with her friends. I stayed home and watched my favorite TV shows. On this night, I was up till Faye got home at 2:00 am. She saw me sitting on the couch.

"You are so boring and have no friends." I looked at her in disgust. "Faye, I do not need to go bar hopping every weekend in my fifties. I am very comfortable with who I am."

"You seem to be going through a gender identity crisis and miserably confused. "You are spending money every weekend. Money, we do not have. My outgoing and bubbly personality was crushed years ago. You depleted all my retirement except the 401K which I promised my ex-husband I would keep for the boys college funds. I insisted my ex-husband take the 40K for his personal use even though it was not stipulated in the divorce. I wish he had, because with the stock market crash, we lost it.

You were on perpetual vacation. No person should be saddled with a spouse like you. Nor should someone experience these difficulties in their marriage and continue to stay in it."

You were hoping I would die so you could cash in on my life insurance policy. You are one sick lazy man. Even when you worked in Maryland at NSA you were up to no good. You were written up several times. I wish I knew all this before I married you.

# The Sweet Sound of Freedom

Life I once knew changed so drastically and was propelling downwards at such a high speed. This made it difficult for me to come to terms with Faye's indiscretions.

Faye was agreeable to see a psychologist only if it helped me admit I was the cause of all the problems in our marriage and not her. The psychologist we picked had to be gay. Faye's initial refusal to see a psychologist with me made it impossible to address any problems in our relationship.

We arrived at our scheduled appointment with the psychologist. When our session began, I spoke up and listed several jobs Jason would be good at and should go after since he was still unemployed.

The psychologist asked Jason what he thought about these jobs. Jason had excuses for why he didn't want to pursue any of the jobs I had provided, including what she suggested. The psychologist lost her patience with Jason and asked. "What the 'F' do you want to do?" "You have a family and kids to support." Jason decided we were not going back to see her anymore even though she wasn't charging us for therapy.

When we were in the parking lot of the psychologist's office, Jason said, "If you want to leave you might as well file for divorce."

I knew my marriage was over and there was no sense in prolonging the misery. I told Jason I wanted a divorce and at first, he didn't agree. He felt we could work this out. Jason knew I did not trust him anymore. I felt very strongly that if you cannot trust your spouse, the marriage is over.

We completed the divorce papers together and I filed for divorce without an attorney. I looked forward to a peaceful life without dealing with Jason or Faye anymore.

It was all over. The divorce was granted, and my marriage of fifteen years was gone in a flash. What a sense of freedom for me. I didn't think I would ever feel this free again. I called Jason up and told him I had just returned from the courthouse. I said. "It's official. We are no longer husband and wife."

# Divorce Celebration

I know I did everything possible to save my marriage to Jason. I was walking away with bittersweet memories. Since I celebrated my marriage fifteen years ago with friends and a party, it was only fitting to celebrate my divorce the same way.

I threw a party celebrating my newfound freedom. I picked the Bar of Bishop to have my party. I invited my friends to join in the celebration. Most of my friends had never heard of a divorce party.

I was so excited on the day of the party. I was going to wear the dress I bought especially for this night. It was a slim clingy dress that showed off my curves. My friends joined me at the bar and celebrated the end of my marriage. Joshua and Jude were at the party too, which made me very happy. They too joined in the celebration. They were excited to see me happy and having a good time after all these years.

The DJ played the song "I am a Survivor" especially for me several times during the night. I danced solo to this song and acted it out. The DJ and my friends were laughing with me and enjoyed seeing me so happy again.

I felt confident that God was with me. He once again snatched me out of a marriage that was no longer good for me. I could feel the presence of the Holy Spirit's arms encircling me with a reassurance that things would be okay from now on.

# Family Update

I have survived being single and have embraced my new 'normal.' I am no longer taking several of the medications I was put on while married to Jason. My illnesses mysteriously disappeared soon after the divorce.

I am raising my bodybuilder friend Stonewall Jackson's grandchildren, whom he adopted. He left them to me in his Will to raise. They are now teenagers who are soon to be fifteen and sixteen. I have my hands full raising them and I treat them no differently than I would my biological sons, Joshua and Jude.

My oldest son, Joshua, bought a home in Carrollton. Texas where he currently lives. It is hard to imagine he is turning 38 years and belongs to the Watermark church in Dallas. He has been there for quite a few years. He is extremely active in the church. He was in a bible study group of men for a few years and enjoyed it. The guys in the group do a lot of outdoor activities like hunting, fishing, and attending bible studies by the lake or just fellowshipping with each other. Jude is turning 36 this year. He keeps busy with his job and hangs around with his friends on weekends watching sports. Both the boys are doing well financially in their jobs and are a great help to me with their younger brother Prince and sister Nasjah.

Right now, both sons have no plans on getting married and told me not to count on grandchildren from them. They feel like I already have grandchildren in Prince and Nasjah.

# Update on Faye

Faye is now in a relationship with another transgender who lives as a man and dresses as a female. To this day Faye will not admit she is gay even though she is in a sexual relationship with a man. I was prescribed estrogen pills after my hysterectomy. The doctor advised me to stop taking them as they made me extremely emotional. Unknown to me, Faye was taking the leftover pills. Faye was bragging to me about developing breasts. By this time, I could not care less what she did, it was none of my business.

I do not have an update on whether Faye is going through any surgical transitions to become a woman. She has legally changed her gender marker to "female" and has changed her driver's license too. We have not spoken to each other since our divorce, and I have no desire to change that.

It is now the year 2025, and I have made the decision to update my book as I have been attending a Bible-Teaching Church. I have found God to be loving, kind, forgiving, and merciful. He wants us to come to Him anytime we are weary and need help!

Jason and I divorced in 2013! Not surprisingly, Faye changed professions and careers several times since our divorce. Ironically, she has been a schoolteacher and a school nurse so she could travel with her boyfriend, who is a teacher during the summer when school is out.

# Afterword

Many women are forced to keep their relationships with their heterosexual cross-dressers or significant others a secret. Not because their husbands or significant others are cross-dressers. But because our society has issues accepting and understanding cross-dressing.

Many heterosexual cross-dressers are living in our country who have chosen to come out of the closet. They have suffered discrimination at the hands of an unaccepting society.

Most heterosexual cross-dressers love and cherish their marriages and relationships with women and children. Jason was the exception to the cross-dressers and gays. His manipulative, passive aggressive behavior is definitely something to be concerned about in future relationships with him.

In most cases, these men do not want to become women. They are secure in their masculine and feminine sides. These were the heterosexual cross-dressers in our first group.

Unfortunately, cross-dressers are discriminated against by their own families. Their families are ashamed of their cross-dressers and choose to cut ties completely with them. Families are more concerned about what their church, friends, and neighbors think when they find out their children are cross-dressers or gays. Parents carry guilt on their shoulders and blame themselves for their kids becoming gay. rather than speaking to their kids first.

This is very important for both cross-dressers and gays as they need love and support from their families. Cross-dressers and gays need to be reminded we have a loving, kind and forgiving God who wants us all to repent for our sins.

I already had a strong relationship with Christ. I sought his guidance through prayer and meditation in this difficult marriage. I firmly believe the Holy Spirit speaks to us in the form of a little voice buried deep down in our core being. He provides us with the answers to our prayers. All we need to do is be still and listen quietly to that voice.

# About the Author

141

Noreen Antao enjoyed a successful sales career in Corporate America, where she honed her communications skills. Her empathy for people suffering injustices. Particularly those whose life is considered taboo by society. Moved her to use those skills to write this book. She is also the biographer who ghostwrote "The Life and Legend of Robert 'Stonewall' Jackson."

Noreen is a Christian Indian whose family came from the State of Goa. India's smallest state. Which is situated on the Arabian Sea. She was born in Karachi. Pakistan. And immigrated to the USA in 1981. Where she immediately went to work in sales. She and her family reside in Texas.